FUNDAMENTALISM
in
American Religion
1880 - 1950

A forty-five-volume facsimile series
reproducing often extremely rare material
documenting the development of one of the
major religious movements of our time

■ *Edited by*
Joel E. Carpenter
Billy Graham Center, Wheaton College

■ *Advisory Editors*
Donald W. Dayton,
Northern Baptist Theological Seminary
George M. Marsden,
Duke University
Mark A. Noll,
Wheaton College
Grant Wacker,
University of North Carolina

A GARLAND SERIES

■ Half a Century
The Autobiography of a Servant

Arno Clemens Gaebelein

Garland Publishing, Inc.
New York & London 1988

For a list of titles in this series, see the final pages of this volume.
This facsimile has been made from a copy at the Moody Bible
Institute

Library of Congress Cataloging-in-Publication Data

Gaebelein, Arno Clemens, 1861-1945.
    Half a century : the autobiography of a servant / Arno
Clemens Gaebelein.
    p. cm. — (Fundamentalism in American religion, 1880-
1950)
    Reprint. Originally published: New York : Publication
office "Our Hope", c1930.
    Includes index.
    ISBN 0-8240-5031-2 (alk. paper)
    1. Gaebelein, Arno Clemens, 1861-1945.   2. Methodist
Church—United States—   Clergy—Biography.   I. Title.   II.
Series.
    BX8495.G23A3 1988
    287' .632'0924—dc 19   88-9789
    [B]   CIP

Design by Valeries Mergentime
Printed on acid-free, 250-year-life paper
Manufactured in the United States of America

EDITOR'S NOTE

■ Arno C. Gaebelein (1861–1945),
a German Methodist pastor, directed a
mission to the Jews in New York's Lower East
Side from 1891 to 1899. He persuaded many
Jews to accept Jesus as Messiah, and
published dozens of widely circulated Yiddish
and Hebrew tracts. Gaebelein founded
Our Hope, a prophecy-oriented monthly, in
1894, and soon became widely acclaimed as a
Bible conference speaker. *Half a Century*
shows Gaebelein's devoted labors and
traces, through his narrative, the growing
fundamentalist network nationwide.

J.A.C.

HALF A CENTURY

A. C. GAEBELEIN IN 1922

Half a Century

THE AUTOBIOGRAPHY
OF A SERVANT

By

ARNO CLEMENS GAEBELEIN
Editor of "Our Hope"

PUBLICATION OFFICE "OUR HOPE"
456 FOURTH AVENUE, NEW YORK, N. Y.
And All Booksellers

CONTENTS

v

FOREWORD

"ALL men of every sort, who have done anything that is meritorious, or that indeed resembles merit, ought, if they be truthful persons and of good report, to set forth their lives with their own hand; but they should not commence so noble an undertaking before they have passed the age of forty years." With these words Benvenuto Cellini began his famous Autobiography. What I have written is not an autobiography. It is the partial record of the greater part of my life spent in the highest possible service, the service for the Lord Jesus Christ, for His Truth and for His Church of which He is the glorified head. There can be nothing higher and nothing more glorious than such a service, a service for God and for man with its inestimable, never-dying fruit.

When the suggestion to write this account was made, I shrank from it. Is it not enough that the Lord knows all about this service, which He in His infinite grace and mercy gave and made possible? We are living in days of self-exaltation and self-glorification. If I should pen the experiences and service of a half of a century, might not this also look like vainglory? While no true servant of Christ boasts of anything, yet would a rehearsal of years of self-sacrificial service not give the impression of boasting?

But one day I perused the many diaries, journals, and other records of long ago. As I wandered once more from place to place, from ocean to ocean, from the bleak Northland to the sunny South, I lived, during these hours, my life over again. And as I read and remembered the great kindness of the Lord, whom I have served in such an imperfect way, His wonderful providences, His guidance, His protection, the many and often startling answers to prayer, and furthermore how graciously He had opened doors and used the ministry of the Gospel and of His Truth in such a remarkable manner, there came to me the conviction that I would not err in writing this book, but on the contrary that it might be wrong to withhold these records from the people of God. And so it became very clear to me that the object of my writing must be to record not what I have done, but what He has done through a weak and erring instrument. With Paul, I should like to put on every page of this volume: "But by the grace of God I am what I am; and His grace which was bestowed upon me was not in vain; but I labored more abundantly than they all; yet not I, but the grace of God which was with me" (1 Cor. xv:10). Even now my heart says—to Him be the glory! All must be and will be unto the praise of the glory of His grace.

What I have to record may also be used for the encouragement of the entire family of God, the household of faith, and especially for the strengthening of the younger servants of Christ, who go forth in ministry, who face the increasing darkness of a passing age, and who labor in the very shadow of the great apostasy.

Needless to say it is impossible to give a full account of fifty years' service, nor can I mention all the fields in which I have been permitted to sow the precious seed.

PART I

THE CALL AND THE BEGINNING

CHAPTER I

IT WAS in 1879 on the last day of October, that
memorable day when the monk of Wittenberg,
Martin Luther, in 1517 hammered his ninety-five
theses to the church door, that I surrendered my
life to the Lord Jesus Christ. This was done in the
city of Lawrence, Massachusetts. A few months
earlier I had arrived in America from the Fatherland. Several years before, that is in my twelfth
year, I had had a definite experience in which I
accepted the Lord Jesus as my Saviour. I left
home for different reasons—one of them was to
escape the compulsory military service—and the
wanderlust was also very strong in me. Before
leaving home, I had spent several hours in a beautiful forest in Thuringia. Unseen by human
eyes I knelt beneath a great hemlock and asked
the Lord to guide me across the ocean, and to show
me the way in which I should go. Often in my
boyhood I had felt a longing to become a foreign
missionary, to preach the Gospel to those who
know it not. The thought came then to me that
my home-leaving might be a stepping-stone
towards that goal.

And so it was that on October 31 in my
eighteenth year I dedicated my young life to the
Lord and asked Him to lead me into His service.

1

This was done without any human instrumentality. I had been reading my New Testament, when suddenly a strong impulse came upon me to seek His presence and to tell Him that work for Him should be my life's work. I had great joy and assurance after my prayer. The desire to become a foreign missionary grew stronger than ever.

I secured employment in a woolen mill at Lawrence. On Lord's day I attended one of the German churches. Shortly after my decision, I came in touch with several Christian men, who had come, a number of years before, from the same principality where I had been brought up. My joy in meeting them was great. They told me that they had a preaching service and a Sunday School, as well as prayer and experience meetings in a small hall. Very readily I accepted their invitation to attend. They were German Methodists. Several of these brethren had done a good deal of service in Germany and on account of their testimony to the Gospel had suffered considerable persecution from the State Church. The first service which I attended was a so-called "Class Meeting." Even now after fifty years this meeting is still vividly remembered. Methodism used to be defined as "Christianity in earnest." Alas! that it is no longer so. When one after the other arose and spoke of the Lord Jesus, how He had washed their sins away, how they enjoyed the peace of

God and knew that they were children of God; when they spoke of their inward joy and their endeavor to win souls for Him and serve Him better, I was melted to tears. And finally I arose and told them of how I knew the same Lord and had yielded my life to Him, that I wanted to be His servant even unto the uttermost parts of the earth. At this they all began to weep for joy.

I could hardly wait for the next Lord's day morning. It was a very small company which had gathered, less than twenty-five. A young man preached, a student from Boston University, Augustus Wallon, son of a godly Methodist preacher of Huguenot stock. He was a year or two older than I was. We became friends at once and for several years had a most intimate fellowship. Often on Saturday evening we would walk for miles and talk over Scripture passages till past midnight and into the early hours of the morning.

With my decision to give my life to the preaching of the Gospel, there came of course the desire to study so as to be fitted for this service. And so I turned to my Latin and Greek grammars and text-books, which we had used in the Gymnasium (the German High School). The declinations and conjugations and everything else now seemed to have become a real pleasure. All my spare hours early in the morning and late at night were used for study and reading.

Then the father of my new found friend, the Presiding Elder, Louis Wallon, came on a quarterly visit. He knew of me, for his son had given him a good report. He had many questions to ask as to my experience, my call to the ministry, the education I had had, and finally he said: "Young brother, I believe the Lord has a work for you; only keep humble and keep close to your Lord." He then recommended the reading and study of certain books which I had not studied before—Church history, a book on systematic theology, and a volume on apologetics. "You can master them yourself," he said. When later some one offered to send me to a theological seminary, Mr. Wallon advised against it. He declared that I knew more Latin and Greek than most graduates of a seminary know. "Keep on in systematic home-study, do not waste your time, and you will be better off in the end." He spoke rightly.

In 1880, after having been received into the membership of the Methodist Episcopal Church, I began my work in earnest. I had a Sunday-School class of small girls, several of whom were led to the Lord through me. I also received an exhorter's license, which was followed some time later by a local preacher's license. I addressed meetings, and the Lord graciously blessed and owned these feeble efforts. The distribution of tracts was also faithfully done, and through it a number of strangers were brought to the services.

4

In 1881 Louis Wallon, in visiting Lawrence again, told me that it had been decided that I should come to New York City. He had received the pastorate of a flourishing German congregation on Second Street. I was to become his assistant and to continue my studies under his supervision. I was overjoyed and could hardly wait till May came, when I would pack my few belongings and enter fully into the Lord's work. When I arrived, I was introduced to Mr. Wallon's father, an excellent Christian. I was to make my home with him. His wife was a godly woman. One of the first things this old Saint did was to put a book in French into my hands. It was *La Future D'Israel* (the future of Israel) by Pasteur Guers. Father Wallon was an ardent Premillennialist, and he tried hard to convert me. But it was too much for me at that time. He talked to me almost daily about the antichrist, the great tribulation, the blessed hope, the kingdom and Israel's future, but I was unable to grasp it. And even his son, who did not share his strong belief in prophecy, cautioned me to beware of such teaching. "Oh," said the old man, "if you only could see this and believe it, and then preach it, how the Lord would use you and bless you." It was all in vain; he could not persuade me to take up the study of prophecy. However, I believe the old saint must have prayed earnestly for me, for six years later the light on unfulfilled

5

prophecy came to me, and one of the first things I did was to order that French book for home study.

My work consisted in making house visitations, calling on the unsaved German people, supplying them with tracts and Bibles, and occasionally addressing meetings in the church. A new mission had been started up-town and I also gave a few days to this field every week. Finally in the fall of this year I was sent every week-end to Bridgeport, Connecticut, to supply a German Methodist Mission there. The Bridgeport Steamboat Company granted me a pass, and so I travelled back and forth for some six or seven months. An officer of the boat whom I asked where to find a furnished room for the week-end told me that he lived in Bridgeport and I could come to his home.

The mission occupied an old store. But few people attended. So I went to work visiting house after house, introducing myself (I am sorry to say with not a little pride) as the new minister of the mission. Soon the attendance doubled and better still people were saved and united with the little church organization. But I was as poor as the proverbial church-mouse. Prayer was my constant refuge; in fact from earliest childhood prayer has always been with me. The first Bible verse I ever learned as a child was Psalm 1:15: "Call upon Me in the time of trouble: I will deliver thee, and thou shalt glorify Me." This blessed verse has never left me. It has become bigger and bigger in my Christian life and experience. It is more real to me now than ever before.

Well I remember how I had saved up, when winter came, to purchase a pair of fine, warm gloves. I was traveling on the Steamer *Laura* to Bridgeport. While in the salon of the steamer I pulled off my precious gloves and put them on a chair. Then I got up to go on deck to look at the lighthouses and watch other boats. All at once I missed my gloves, and when I went back where I left them, they were gone. What could I do? Well, I used my verse, turned to a little dark nook and prayed earnestly. After a few minutes I returned to the part of the boat where I had left them and here they were. The unknown person who had taken my gloves had put them back on the same chair. Similar experiences came to me. One stormy day my hat blew away, and when I regained it in a badly damaged condition I felt that I could hardly wear it for the Sunday services. I had no money and as I never borrowed money from anybody, I prayed about it. A short time after, the same day, a person who had attended several services in the mission, came and handed me some money with the statement, "This is for yourself, you probably need it." Some may smile at the simplicity of all this. But this prayer habit, to take even the smallest things to Him who cares for us has never left me. When we think of Him in the last chapter of the Gospel of John, how His blessed hands which had been nailed to the cross gathered sticks, kindled a fire, and prepared a breakfast for His toiling servants, can we ever doubt His loving interest in the smallest affairs of our little lives?

All along I was hard at work studying and reading, fairly devouring and absorbing book after book. My mind then and for years after became like a great reservoir stored with all kinds of knowledge. I was young and blessed with a remarkable memory. What I acquired in my philological, theological, philosophical studies and the reading of choice literature in several languages during my youth, has remained with me through life, and now approaching the three score and ten line, I know nothing of an impaired memory. During the winter of 1881-1882 I also prepared myself for admission to the Methodist Conference as a regular member, for it had been decided that I should do this.

The Conference session was held in the city of Baltimore, Maryland. The East German Conference consisted at that time of about thirty-five members and Bishop Wiley presided over it. The examination committee gave a most flattering report of my attainments, so much so that the Bishop thought it was most remarkable, took me by the hand, and wished me the Lord's blessing and great success. All along I knew nothing of what field of labor I would receive. Finally something was whispered, but I did not know of my appointment till the Bishop read the list, and I learned that I was to have charge of a small congregation on Harford Avenue in Baltimore. The different members of the Conference all wished me God speed. They were all godly and able men, of an entirely different stamp from some of the Methodist ministry today. So far as I know only one of these men is left, living in retirement. All have gone to their reward. I hold them in loving memory.

Returning to my lodgings at Grandfather Wallon's simple home, I soon packed my belongings, consisting mostly of books, and set out for Baltimore. My predecessor, John Lutz, who came to meet me at the old President Street Station, and who became my life-long friend, welcomed me heartily. He took me round to meet the different members of the congregation, secured an excellent home for me, and assisted me in various other ways. The first sermon I preached was on Romans xv:29, "And I am sure that, when I come unto you, I shall come in the fulness of the blessing of the Gospel of Christ."

But while I knew the Gospel and knew God's salvation, yet how very little of it all I knew then. The glorious heights of the Gospel as revealed in the Ephesian Epistle were unknown to me. The knowledge of the Gospel has been throughout my life and ministry an ever-expanding knowledge. I fear that those who speak of the mastery of the Gospel, as if the Gospel were the most simple thing in our Christian faith, have never looked deep enough. It is very true that the Gospel of our salvation is very simple, yet there are depths which no saint has ever fathomed. Not until we reach the Father's house in everlasting glory shall we know the fulness of the Gospel.

Baltimore became at once a beloved spot to me. My lodging place was outside of the city limits, on Harford Road, restful and very congenial. The members of the congregation were very hospitable and kind, and bore patiently with their young and inexperienced preacher. As I was boyish-looking, they called me the boy-preacher. I also brushed against some young American people with whom, ten and fifteen years later, I formed a close friendship. Little did I think then that Baltimore would later take a prominent place in my enlarged ministry.

As my congregation was small and there was little visiting to be done, I had ample time to devote to study. The call to the foreign field came up again and again, and with this in view I devoted a great deal of time to the study of languages. I was especially drawn to the Semitic group of languages. A year before I had begun the study of Hebrew, but now with much time on my hands, I fairly plunged into study. Grammars, dictionaries and reading books in six or seven languages were bought. For many months I arose every morning at four and put in three hours of solid study before breakfast. Every spare hour during the day was used in the same way. I carried with me little note-books in which were written Hebrew, Aramaic, Arabic, Syriac and Persian verbs, nouns, adjectives and sentences. If I had to wait for somebody, or even while I was walking on the street, out came the little note-book. Professor Paul Haupt had come at that time from the University of Goettingen to teach Semitic languages in Johns Hopkins. While I was attending one of his classes, he wrote some Arabic words on the black board and asked the class to read. I read them off readily, and he wanted to know where I had been taught Arabic. When I told him that I had taught myself, he looked rather dubious.

With all this intensive study, my pastoral work was not neglected. In a few months the audiences had more than doubled, so that the chapel was filled to its full capacity. The Lord blessed the preaching of the Gospel in the salvation of not a few.

It was in the second year of my ministry in Baltimore that I made my first attempt at writing

11

for publication in the German language. I had made a trip to the Luray Caverns and I selected these Virginia caves as the topic of my maiden effort. It pleased so much that I was asked to write other articles for the same German Monthly. Later I wrote German devotional studies as well as articles exposing "Christian Science," and for several years I was the New York correspondent for a German religious weekly, *The Apologist*.

The time limit for the Methodist Ministry in the 80's was three years. As I had had a phenomenal success in my Baltimore charge and had been there only two years, I fully expected to remain for the third year. When the Conference of 1884 came, having received my ordination as a deacon, I was informed that I would have to leave Baltimore and take charge of a New York congregation. It was a great surprise. It was hard to leave Baltimore and the many friends I had made.

CHAPTER II

M Y NEW field was the upper part of New York,
known as Harlem. It was but sparsely
settled at that time. Big stretches of farm lands
with green meadows, fine vegetable gardens with
numerous rocky elevations, were seen in every
direction. The territory was not unknown to
me, for I had done some work there in 1881,
visiting here and there, and inviting people to
attend the first services, which had been started
about that time. As Harlem was rapidly building
up, a church building had been erected on One
Hundred and Fourteenth Street near Third
Avenue. There was a heavy debt on the building,
and my first work was to remove this debt. This
was generally done by having the preacher in
charge visiting the different congregations in the
conference, presenting the need, and then taking
the Conference Church Erection Collection. The
Presiding Elder and the older members took me
aside and impressed upon me that it was a
great distinction for so young a man (I was in
my twenty-third year) to be entrusted with
such a responsible undertaking. I knew the
Lord would prosper me in it, for I prayed much
and felt sure of His blessing. A good part of
the year was taken up with traveling, and all the

needed funds had been secured by the end of the year. Besides preaching in the different congregations, I also gave an interesting lecture which was much appreciated.

But the year 1884 became one of the outstanding years of my life for another reason. The Presiding Elder, C. F. Grimm, a godly and able, as well as honored Methodist preacher, when I had difficulty in obtaining suitable lodgings, was kind enough to open his home and invite me to stay there till I could locate the proper place to live. His family was most remarkable. It consisted of nine daughters and two sons. And they were a happy family. It is not hard for the reader to guess the rest of the story. Among the young ladies was one with a happy face. She attracted my attention, and before many weeks had passed Emma promised to become my wife. Later we confessed to each other that it was love at first sight. It is written "Whoso findeth a wife findeth a good thing, and obtaineth favor of the Lord" (Prov. xviii:22) and "a prudent wife is of the Lord" (Prov. xix:14). Next to salvation I consider her, the wife of my youth, the greatest gift of the Lord, and all the work I have been privileged in doing must be credited, at least in part, to her faithfulness and loving, as well as sacrificial, assistance. Accustomed to a minister's life, she knew the hardships of it. Well trained by a good mother in

14

A. C. GAEBELEIN IN 1882

household duties, she knew how to manage a home. Pleasing in every way yet never forward, always unassuming, thinking first of my comfort and the comfort and well-being of others, she has been entirely unselfish. With her thrift she made an excellent home, though often the slender means hardly reached to meet our needs. When later my ocean to ocean ministry developed, one of her favored phrases became, "Do not consider me in the least; do whatever you think you should do; the Lord will take care." How many times it happened when I was far away, serving on some Western prairie, or in the far Northland, that sickness came into the home. The children were ill, or she was sick. But many times it was kept secret until recovery had taken place, and then I was told "not to trouble or disturb you in your work, I did not write you about it." How different my life would have been, if I had not had this priceless gift!

A year later we married and founded an humble home next to the church. The Lord crowned my efforts with blessing. Numerous young people were led to Christ. The Sunday audiences increased. I also continued in my studies and in my literary activities in the German. Then the Lord sent us a dear little baby girl to crown our happiness. But she was a gift for a short time only. I called her "my little pilgrim"; though she was only a five-months-old, whenever I called her by this name she gave me a happy smile. One day she did not smile, and a few days later her little blood-redeemed soul had fled, and she was "Safe in the arms of Jesus, safe on His gentle breast." It was our first great sorrow, but He carried us through.

I began to be greatly troubled. Did the Lord permit this sudden home-call to remind me of my desire, if not call, to go to some foreign land or foreign people to preach the Gospel? This desire had always been before me. The study of different oriental languages, which I still kept up, was done with this in view. My wife knew all about it. At that time a small volume was put into my hand, *The Crisis of Missions*, by Dr. Arthur T. Pierson. I devoured it, and little did I think that eighteen years later I should number Dr. Pierson among my best friends and labor with him in different parts of the country and in Bible Conferences. I told him later how his excellent book fired my soul afresh to go to the regions beyond and to preach the Gospel where Christ's name was not mentioned. I prayed earnestly and waited for providential leadings, which never seemed to come.

My three years having expired in the Harlem congregation and having been ordained in 1886 as an Elder in the Methodist Episcopal Church, I had to move to another field. Different congregations had asked for me, but since I had preached in the German Methodist Church of Hoboken, N. J., across the Hudson River, the official Board of that Church, composed of New York business men, insisted that I become their pastor. This was a larger congregation and we found a great and happy welcome. Besides the church in Hoboken, another mission had been started in West Hoboken, which I supplied, and a few years later we built a church there also. The Lord increasingly blessed my ministry of the Gospel. Many were saved in the different protracted meetings I held. Among them was an entire Dalmatian or Croatian family. One of the sons became a successful preacher, and his oldest son is also preaching the Gospel in London, England. One interesting experience I must relate. In making calls in different tenement houses, whenever I found closed doors, I left a little tract. One day a Roman Catholic woman was saved and when she bore testimony of her salvation, she mentioned the fact that her attention was arrested first of all by a little tract which bore my name and address.

The missionary call did not leave me. I was still waiting for His leading. Finally I began to correspond with Dr. James M. Thoburn, later Bishop Thoburn. After I had met this remarkable man, who had been so widely used in India and after I had had a lengthy interview with him, he said at once: "You are the man we want and need." He told me that he was looking for a principal to take charge of an Anglo-Chinese School in Singapore and thought I was fitted for it. Then he mentioned the possibility of starting a mission in Batavia in the island of Java and spoke of other openings. My old enthusiasm came back, and the negotiations went so far that Dr. Thoburn requested the Bishop to grant me a transfer.

But then arose the difficulties. The older brethren did not see eye to eye with me at all. They made serious objections. My wife declared herself willing to go with little Paul, born in 1887, though she felt no call to the foreign field. Much prayer and waiting on the Lord followed, but when finally a physician declared that my wife would not live very long in a tropical climate, though she was in perfect health, I felt that all negotiations should stop. To this Dr. Thoburn agreed.

A short time after, something of great importance happened which ultimately led to the work in which the Lord has so graciously and greatly blessed me. In the congregation I served was a converted Hebrew, Samuel Goldstein, who acted as an interpreter in connection with the immigration office in New York. One day, being in my library, he looked over my books, and when he saw books in Hebrew and other Semitic languages, he asked if I understood Hebrew. When I took down a Hebrew Bible and read to him, he

A. C. GAEBELEIN IN 1896

WITNESSING TO ISRAEL

ɔurst out, saying, "It is a shame that you do not make use of your knowledge. You should do a greater work than preaching to a German congregation." I told him that my studies since 1882 had been in Semitic and Oriental languages, because I felt called to go to the Orient to preach the Gospel there. He answered, "There is an Orient and there are thousands of foreigners right over here in New York; Jews are coming in by the thousands from every European and several Oriental countries. You should go and preach the Gospel to the Jews. I believe the Lord made you take up these studies because He wants you to go to my brethren, the Jews."

I did not see it at once in this light. But the good brother persisted. When I told him that I did not think that Jews would come and listen to a Gentile preacher, he urged me to make a trial. To this I consented readily.

Now there was at that time a Hebrew Christian Mission on St. Marks Place, conducted by Jacob Freshman, the son of a Jewish Rabbi. It was arranged on a certain Saturday afternoon that I should address an audience of Jews in the German language. I do not know how much advertising was done, but a fine and respectful audience greeted me. I spoke for about thirty-five minutes on the prophecies of a suffering Messiah, the true Lamb of God. The attention was remarkable. They were deeply interested.

I thought perhaps it was the novelty of a Gentile speaking to them and quoting Hebrew sentences, but having promised to speak again the next Saturday afternoon, I found even a larger gathering. Some came to me with their questions, which seemed to indicate a spirit of genuine inquiry after the truth. My friend, Samuel Goldstein, was very enthusiastic and predicted great things. I continued to speak regularly at Mr. Freshman's place for about a year.

This initial attempt to bring the Gospel to the Jews led me deeper into the Old Testament Scriptures. I began to study prophecy. Up to this time I had followed in the interpretation of Old Testament prophecy the so-called "spiritualizing method." Israel, that method teaches, is no longer the Israel of old, but it means the Church now. For the natural Israel no hope of a future restoration is left. All their glorious and unfulfilled promises find now their fulfillment in the Church of Jesus Christ. But as I came in closer touch with this remarkable people, those who are still orthodox, I soon had to face their never-dying hope. As I began to read their *Machsorim*, their rituals and prayers, I found the expressions of hope and longing for Messiah's coming. Do they not say each time *Pesach* is celebrated, commemorating their supernatural deliverance out of Egypt's slavery, "This year here, next year in Jerusalem"? Many an old, long-bearded, orthodox Hebrew assured me that the Messiah, the Son of David, the Bethlehemite, will surely come to claim David's throne. In the beginning it sounded foreign to me, but as I turned to the Bible I soon discovered the real hope of Israel and the truth of the promised return of our Lord, and the earthly glories connected with that future event were brought through the Spirit of God to my heart. Then the study of the Bible became my most fascinating occupation, and as I continued in my search, I knew that the Lord wanted me to turn aside from the regular ministry and devote myself to work among God's ancient people. Now all seemed to become clear as to why the Lord prevented my going to the regions beyond. He had a work for me to do among the thousands who were arriving month after month in our great American Metropolis. They came mostly from Russia where they were so cruelly persecuted and were indeed "like sheep without a shepherd." Misery and want were seen everywhere on the East side of New York where they mostly settled. And my heart, like His great heart, was deeply moved with compassion.

PART II

THE TESTIMONY TO ISRAEL

CHAPTER III

MY PASTORATE in Hoboken having terminated, I rejected the pastorate of another Church in New York and requested the Bishop to appoint me to work among the Jews. So we moved to New York; my wife, Paul, four years and Arno, one year old. I was to continue in Mr. Freshman's work. After several months of successful preaching my attention was called to the Allen Street Memorial Methodist Episcopal Church in Rivington Street. This church was famous more than two generations ago on account of its great revivals in which hundreds and thousands were brought to the knowledge of the Lord. But now the English speaking people had moved away, and the entire neighborhood was thickly settled with Russian, Polish, Austrian and Roumanian Jews. The Allen Memorial was in an excellent location to reach these strangers who had come to our shores. I saw the pastor, Mr. William Hamilton, who readily granted the permission for me to use the church Saturday afternoons to preach to the Jews. On the day before the Jewish Sabbath, when thousands were passing, I wrote in Hebrew characters on a piece of cardboard the following: "Tomorrow, Sabbath afternoon at 3 o'clock, a German Gentile preacher, who knows Hebrew and is a friend of Israel will give a lecture on the Bible." The announcement was displayed in the window. I came half an hour before the set time, and as I turned the corner I saw the men streaming into the building, and long before the hour arrived we had to close the doors, the place being filled. I do not remember what I preached about, but the audience was deeply interested.

When I was through, my hearers crowded around me. Some thanked me for the words spoken, others had questions to ask, and many more demanded literature in Yiddish or Hebrew. All seemed to be pleased when I announced that these Saturday services would be continued. When the next Jewish Sabbath-day arrived, the lecture room seating about five hundred was over-crowded, and I had once more a most attentive audience. A few weeks later we were forced to open the larger auditorium, which seated over fifteen hundred. Many times every seat was taken. It was an impressive sight to see over a thousand Jews, long-bearded orthodox Jews, and many young men gathering week after week to listen to a Gentile preacher, preaching from their Old Testament about Christ, their long-promised Messiah. But soon a strong spirit of antagonism developed in these meetings. Almost in every service there were interruptions. After I had preached to them for about two months, some well-versed, shrewd Hebrews had questions about what the Gentile preacher said. I never objected to these interruptions, but stopped my discourse and listened to them. Then came my answer and whenever it displeased my questioner, or I had met his argument in favor of our Lord, the man would get up again, and, instead of addressing me, he would address the audience, his own brethren. Waving his hands excitedly, as only a Jew can, he would say something like this, "Why are you listening to a *Goji* (Gentile) to tell you that the one whom they hanged is Messiah? Get out of here! Get up and leave! Come on!" The crowd responded generously and many times I was left with only a hundred who were willing to listen to the rest of my discourse. I give an illustration of the questions that were asked.

Once a Rabbi got up and asked to be heard. When I gave him the privilege, he said the following: "You have told us that your Jesus is now doing what our Aaron did as high priest; that Jesus is the priest through whom we are represented before God. But tell me, Mr. Preacher, how can your Jesus be a priest when he is of the tribe of Judah! To be a priest he must be of Levi." He looked about triumphantly. I answered him by quoting in Hebrew a verse from the one hundred and tenth Psalm, "Thou art a Priest forever after the order of Melchisedec," and then I told them that their ancient and scholarly Rabbis had interpreted this verse as meaning the Messiah, that Messiah would be a Priest and a King. I used the argument of the seventh chapter of the Epistle to the Hebrews. The questioning Rabbi sat down and behaved very well for a few moments, but finally he got up and left, followed by a hundred or more of my hearers. Yet when the next Sabbath came the same crowd gathered again.

These services were held in a very simple way. For a time I attempted congregational singing. It proved a failure. I reminded them of their first national song recorded in the fifteenth chapter of Exodus and its connection with redemption. I quoted to them from Psalm 137:

> By the rivers of Babylon we sat down
> Yea, we wept, when we remembered Zion.
> We hanged our harps upon the willows
> In the midst thereof.
> For there they that had carried us away captive,
> Required of us a song of mirth, saying;
> Sing us one of the songs of Zion.
> How shall we sing the Lord's song
> In a strange land?

I told them of passages in prophecy which speak of their future songs of joy, when Messiah comes, and they are gathered back to their old home-land, and that now they too could learn to sing the song of redemption by trusting the Lamb of God.

28

The service was opened with prayer. Occasionally we had several Gospel songs sung by a Christian believer. Then came the reading of the Scriptures, which covered the same portion of the Pentateuch which was read in the synagogues. My discourse lasted frequently for an hour and sometimes longer. A closing prayer ended the service.

During the winter of 1892 I preached a series of ten sermons on "Joseph and His Brethren." They made a deep impression and I had to repeat them for several years. So great was the interest that I published them in very large editions. These addresses have gone forth in many thousands of copies in English, German, Yiddish, Hebrew, Arabic, Swedish, Dutch, Polish, Russian, Spanish and Bohemian.

Early in this testimony to the Jewish people I started a room for inquirers. It was one of the Sunday School Class Rooms of the Allen Street Memorial Church. I opened this room daily during certain hours of the afternoon. On the table I put several Hebrew Bibles and the Hebrew New Testament translated by Prof. Franz Delitzsch, also German and English booklets. I soon had the joy of meeting several serious inquirers, but they were very few. Many others came, but it did not take me long to discover that selfish motives prompted them in their inquiries. How many young men came and asked something like this: "If I become a Christian and get baptized, do you think Christians will help me to become educated as a physician, a dentist, or can I become a preacher?" Needless to say that they did not approach me the second time with such questions.

The accusation from the side of intelligent Hebrews, that the Jewish Missions have encouraged such a miserable spirit and these mercenary motives in order to make converts, is not wholly unfounded. Many of the converts of certain Missions conducted by Jewish converts are nothing but hirelings and a disgrace to both Judaism and Christianity. Yet there have been and there are genuine cases of real conversion. I saw a number of such where there was more than a mental persuasion that Jesus of Nazareth is Israel's true Messiah. There was a real conviction of sin, true repentance and faith in the Lord Jesus Christ, and the lives of these Hebrew brethren bore witness to the fact that they had been born again. One of the joys of this ministry to the Jewish people has been the fact that many years later I heard from Jews who accepted the Lord Jesus Christ as Saviour and who told me that one of my sermons preached at 91 Rivington Street had started them towards a true Christian experience. Only recently, nearly forty years after, in preaching in one of our New York churches, a well-dressed man approached me, asking if I am the same Pastor Gaebelein who used to preach in Rivington Street.

He then said, "I heard you preach then and I believe now what you preached."

The increasing attendance in the services and the fact that a Gentile preacher had the ear of thousands of Jews attracted wide-spread attention. During the winter of 1892-1893 a Saturday morning service was held. This service, conflicting with the services in the different synagogues, was not as largely attended as the afternoon meetings, and only the most interested came. Dr. Richard Wheately, Editor of the *Pittsburgh Christian Advocate* at that time, a scholar, who understood the German language, attended one of these services on Saturday morning. We quote what he wrote about it in his paper:

> "On Saturday morning May 5, the writer listened to an eloquent and powerful sermon in the Allen Street Memorial Church, located on Rivington Street, from the Rev. A. C. Gaebelein. About two hundred and fifty well dressed, intelligent Jews—the average number in constant attendance, paid strictest heed to the discourse. Well they might, for every gesture was vocal with thought and feeling and in harmony with the finely modulated voice. More than that, the power, the utterance, reiterated by the great Apostle to the Gentiles was in every sentence. The speaker was intensely in earnest. Most of his receptive and yet critical hearers were absorbed in what he said, and none could be more orderly and yet more free in movement. Many of them were orthodox, men of thought, desiring clear views on religion."

Preachers of different denominations, editors of periodicals, educators and others having heard of the phenomenal work, came to see for themselves what was done. Among these were Bishop Andrews of the Methodist Church, several editors of Methodist papers, influential laymen, among whom may be mentioned John S. Huyler, Bowles Colgate, Samuel Bowen, and others.

It became evident after this work had been carried on for almost a year, that the greatest need was for suitable literature. The Jewish people love to read and there was a constant cry for something to read. I gave myself to increased study of Hebrew literature and Hebrew customs and traditions. The Hebrew Orthodox prayer books for all the great feasts were carefully studied as well as talmudical writings. I literally massacred my good classical German and acquired the "Yiddish," which means that you make as many grammatical errors as you possibly can, and use a good sprinkling of Hebrew words and expressions. I mastered it so well that, when I visited Buffalo and gathered a company of Jews in a hall, addressing them in Yiddish, after I had spoken a few minutes, one of them arose and demanded to be heard. He said: "Why have you to lie and be ashamed of your nationality? Here you started and said that you are a Gentile and now we all hear with our own ears that you are a Jew, just as we are." Fortunately a German Pastor was in the audience, and he arose in my defense.

Then I also learned to use the Hebrew script

to correspond with Hebrews and to write articles for publication.

At the same time I started in earnest to produce a Yiddish Gospel literature. In 1893 began the publication of *Tiqweth Israel—The Hope of Israel Monthly*. It had in the first year only eight pages, but was soon increased to sixteen and then twenty-four pages. I wrote nearly everything myself in Hebrew script. It created a great impression among the Jews and is mentioned in the "Jewish Encyclopedia." We printed first 5,000 copies each month, but several times we issued 15,000, and they were in great demand. Not only were they freely circulated in our New York Ghetto, but they were sent to friends of Israel in most of our large cities and hundreds of copies were mailed to Eastern Europe. When I visited Russia three years later, I found how graciously this written testimony had been used. Coming to Kieff I had promised to address some Jews in that "holy city," but I did not know any of them. When the train rolled into the station, several men were on the platform holding high my *Tiqweth Israel*. In Roumania I visited a forsaken mountain town just to meet one Jew, who had read my paper and had written me some good letters.

Besides publishing "Joseph and His Brethren" in enormous editions, I wrote numerous tracts and booklets. The Mildmay Mission to the

Jews in London published in 1905 a complete catalogue of "Christian Tracts for Jewish Readers." This catalogue credits me with the following booklets: "Messiah and His People Israel," "Israel's Awakening," "Prophecies Relating to Christ," "Zechariah's Prophecy," "Israel's Hoffnung," "The Meaning of Zionism," "Mi Hu Ze?" (Who is this?), "Ruach HaQodesh" (The Holy Spirit), "Shalom Alechem" (Peace Be Unto You), "Shalom al Arez" (Peace on Earth), "Tephilath Zadikim Yishma" (The Hearing of the Prayer of the Righteous), "Yom Ha-shelishi" (The Third Day). But this list is not complete; at least six other Yiddish tracts were written and published by me.

The authorities of the Methodist Episcopal Church, including Bishop Andrews, had now been aroused to the great possibilities of evangelizing the Jewish masses in down-town New York. Having taken a transfer to the New York East Conference, I became identified with the New York City Church Extension and Missionary Society of the Methodist Episcopal Church, Dr. Frank Mason North, Secretary. The work increased steadily; the attendance at the public meetings continued very large. New services were added, especially one on Lord's day afternoons. Several intelligent Hebrews confessed Christ, and I baptized them. A believers' meeting was also started.

Immigration being unrestricted at that time

brought many thousands of Jews to America. Many of them came from Russia and Poland, where they had suffered such cruel persecutions. Times were hard in the early nineties; breadlines and soup-kitchens were plentiful, and I was obliged to do something for the relief of the great suffering among the poor Jews. It appeared to me a grand opportunity to show to them the practical side of Christianity. I had a visitor who went through the tenement houses, and numerous families were found on the verge of starvation. I appealed to wholesale grocery and commission houses to send barrels of potatoes, flour, etc., to the church building, and there was a generous response. We could help hundreds of Jewish families in their abject poverty. Many times I denied myself the most necessary things in order to help them in their distress, and many times I felt great joy and His approval in loving and helping the suffering members of the people who are still His people. I could do just a little in paying back the debt we owe to the Jews. How true Christians can have no heart for the Jew, or even ignore and despise him, is hard to understand. I doubt not that through this relief work, through words of kindness and sympathy, some hearts were touched and perhaps opened to the Gospel, which was never omitted when relief was given.

When the Jewish holidays came, *Rosh Hashonah* and *Yom Kippur*, the New Year and the Day of

Atonement, I always held special services. It was surprising that even on their most holy day, the Day of Atonement, a day of strictest fasting and prayer, hundreds of Jews came to listen to the Gentile preacher and what he had to say about atonement. I always called at such occasions the attention of orthodox Hebrews to a most significant paragraph in their prayers on the Day of Atonement. I quote it:

"We have fallen into sin, still Thou hast not become tired of us, *though Messiah our righteousness has turned away from us*, and we are full of fear, because there is none to justify us. *He* (Messiah) has borne the yoke of iniquities, He is wounded for our sins, He carries our transgressions upon His shoulders, that He may find pardon for our iniquities. We shall be healed by His wounds." I quoted this most remarkable prayer in speaking to them on the fifty-third chapter of Isaiah. It was on the Day of Atonement that I held each year a special meeting with believing Hebrews. One of these early services I shall never forget. A dozen or so gathered and we remembered the Lord in the breaking of bread. We all felt His blessed nearness in that simple service.

As the work enlarged it became evident that it could not be confined to a denomination. The City Mission paid me a salary, furnished the building, but the need for tons of Christian literature, assistants in the work, etc., had to be met through other sources. I was cast upon the Lord for these needs and He set His gracious approval upon my efforts. The City Mission authorities realized this at once. They felt that this movement must be free to develop on such lines as will prevent all denominational narrowness. I quote their own statements: "The New York City Church Extension and Missionary Society of the Methodist Episcopal Church has for nearly two years given special attention to this problem (the Hebrew population in down-town New York) as it confronts us in this city, and for a large part of that time has fostered the work which is outlined in the report of its able representative, Rev. A. C. Gaebelein. By opening one of its best churches to the large and frequent services, by providing the necessary support of Mr. Gaebelein, and by the coöperation of its other workers and officers with him in this effort, it has promoted and sustained this unique and interesting work as earnestly as possible. With the present year it has put the movement upon a stronger footing. The large and the roomy house, 209 Madison Street, becomes the headquarters of the work. A representative committee, composed of Messrs. Bowles Colgate, Hiram Merritt, the Rev. Drs. G. H. Gregory, W. H. Wardell and C. S. Harrower, supervise the work and the financial management. *The enlargement of the work, however, and its increased efficiency must depend upon the voluntary offerings of the Friends of Israel.* We ask their attention to the spirit, method, and promise of this special effort we are making to bring the Jewish multitude of our city to know the living Christ and to receive the Holy Spirit.

"The Rev. A. C. Gaebelein, who is intrusted with the leadership of this movement, is rarely endowed for the responsibility. Himself a German—a Gentile—scholarly, devout, an effective speaker, a painstaking pastor, he has already won success in the regular work of the East German Conference. Now after the study of the Hebrew language and literature and of Biblical Prophecy, and with a profound conviction that he is called to this service, he devotes himself to the chosen people of God, and is already recognized far and wide as their friend.

"He is a member of the New York East Conference of the Methodist Episcopal Church, yet within *certain well-defined limits he is free to develop this Mission on such broad lines as will prevent all denominational narrowness.*"

The name selected for this work was *The Hope of Israel Movement.* The blessed word "Hope" became thus early the leading word. It is still so. The Lord Jesus Christ is "Our Hope", the Hope of His Church, the Hope of Israel, the Hope of the World.

CHAPTER IV

THE FRIENDS of Israel were beginning to take notice of the work which was being done among God's ancient people. Among those who became very much interested were the noble witnesses of the Niagara Bible Conference movement. Under the leadership of that stalwart champion of the Truth of God, a giant in Bible knowledge and Bible teaching, Dr. James H. Brookes, Pastor of the Washington Avenue Presbyterian Church, St. Louis, Missouri, summer Bible Conferences had been held for about twelve years. His associates were Drs. Nathanael West, W. J. Erdman and his brother Albert, Professor Morehead, A. J. Gordon, George C. Needham, J. M. Stifler, Arthur T. Pierson, Dr. Parsons, C. I. Scofield and others. All these beloved brethren, who are no longer here, showed a lively interest in my work. Dr. Brookes was the Editor of *The Truth*. We shall never forget our first meeting together. It was in the presence of Professor Morehead of Xenia, Ohio. Knowing that I was German and being suspicious of German rationalism, he made me pass an examination. He wanted to know what I believed about the authorship of the Pentateuch, whether it was Mosaic or documentary. Then came questions about the Book of Isaiah, the authenticity of Daniel, and the historicity of Jonah. Finally Dr. Brookes turned to Morehead and said, "He is all right!" He took me literally under his wings. The next issue of his monthly brought a splendid endorsement of myself and the work. And a few months later he mentioned the work again. He said: "Mr. Gaebelein is a German, a Gentile, an accomplished scholar, who feels called of God to the work of preaching the Gospel to the Jews; and already the Lord has set His approval upon the ministry of His servant. The following private letter, just received from him and published without his knowledge tells its own story."

Since I last wrote, still larger numbers of Israelites have come to hear me preach. Thus on the 4th, the Secretary of the City Mission counted 592 in attendance while I was speaking. The Jews who attend my services are mostly from the orthodox class. About four months ago I had more of the rationalistic class, but finding that I would not debate with them, they dropped off, and now only the God-fearing, Bible-loving, and prophecy-believing (though so blind) attend my services. What do you think of the following conversation, after an explanation of Isa. vii:14? *Rationalistic Jew*: "Pastor, how is it possible that a virgin could conceive without a man and how could the Son of God be born?" *Myself*: "Do you believe in God?" *Jew*: "Yes, in some kind of a higher power." *Myself*: "Do you believe that, according to the account of Moses, God created man out of the dust of the earth, and do you believe that Sarah gave birth to Isaac in her *old* age?" *Jew*: "*Never*; Moses never wrote anything, and all you say is myth." *Myself*: "Very well; if you do not be-

40

lieve this, it is all in vain for me to talk with you; Good bye."

This class I got rid of, and I have now the largest Jewish *orthodox* audiences in the city. . . . Your heart would be made glad, if you could listen to some of the conversations I have with these orthodox Jews. *Oh! how they look for the coming of the Messiah, and how they expect Him soon!—* much more so than our Christian people, even those who believe in His coming; and then when they hear my words, and see my faith in the coming reign of their Messiah, their faces light up, and it is so easy to convince them of His first appearance in Bethlehem, according to Micah v:1: Praise the Lord that He has filled my soul with "that blessed hope," enabling me to be a witness of it to the Jew. Don't you think that the reason of so many failures in Jewish mission work is simply in not preaching the *whole* truth?

While the work in Rivington Street, and in the Madison Street house constantly increased, I also visited other places outside of New York to give the Jews the Gospel. In the southern part of New Jersey had been started the Baron Hirsch Colonies for Jews. There were numerous settlements, the most prominent being Rosenhayn and Alliance. A devoted Christian lady, Miss Snow, had gone there to live and I made several visits, gathering the Jewish farmers and preaching to them. But it was difficult work. One of these visits I shall never forget. I left on a cold winter morning to go to Rosenhayn. It was at a time when I could hardly afford the extra expense of traveling. Printer's bills were due and several hundred dollars were needed. A few dollars were all my belongings. It was bitter cold, but I had a score or more of hearers who paid good attention to the address. The meeting ended. I hardly knew what to do. Vineland was the nearest place, six miles away. I was about to start on my journey when a Jew asked me to come to his shack. I climbed a ladder to the attic and found a hard bed close to the window with hardly enough covering for a temperature of five below Zero. I shivered all night long and discovered in the morning that the window was minus the glass. Then I walked back to Vineland and took the train for home. But I was worried about those printers bills and the money needed. When I reached home tired and hungry, my wife met me with a smile and said, "I have a big surprise for you. This parcel came yesterday by registered mail." I opened it and found a book inside with a note unsigned, asking me to read the book, because I would find something between its pages which I could use as I pleased. In going through the volume I found fifty ten dollar bills—five hundred dollars. All need was met. Many such experiences were mine over and over again in answer to prayer.

During 1893 I also met for the first time Dr. A. B. Simpson. He had started a few years before the Christian Alliance movement, and, while I could not fully endorse his teaching on "divine healing," I accepted his invitation to speak in the Gospel Tabernacle and in different conventions. Later Dr. Arthur T. Pierson and myself were for a short time trustees of the Christian and Missionary Alliance. I also supplied for several years Jewish Notes and Notes on Prophecy for *The Alliance Magazine*. This opened many new doors and acquainted hundreds of Christians with the work I was doing. I made for several years periodical visits, month after month to Pittsburgh, where a branch of the Hope of Israel had been opened. My meetings were held in different United Presbyterian Churches, and the Lord's blessing rested upon the testimony I gave concerning Israel's hope so vitally linked with the return of our Lord. I also visited Boston for the first time. My first public address was delivered in the Park Street Congregational Church, where seven years later I started the Boston Monthly Meetings for Boston and vicinity, which are still being held by me, entering now upon the thirty-first season. In the same year I met Dr. Reuben A. Torrey for the first time in New Haven, Connecticut (1894). A big convention was held, and he presided over the meeting which I had been asked to address on "The Jews and Their Future." Every once in a while a subdued "Amen" came from his lips, and when I had finished Torrey said: "I am glad you told them about the Coming of the Lord; they don't know much about this around here."

During the summer of 1893 Professor Ernst
F. Stroeter, Ph. D., visited New York and attended
one of my Saturday services. Dr. Stroeter was
professor in the Denver (Colorado) University;
an able scholar and Christian gentleman and above
everything an ardent believer in prophecy, the
premillennial Coming of the Lord, and the restoration of Israel. While I preached, the tears
were streaming down his face and one could
see how deeply he was moved. I had met him
before. His first question was: "Do you think
there would be a place for me in this work? I
will gladly resign my professorship in Denver
and join you in this glorious work." What he
suggested materialized the following year, and
he became the Secretary of the Hope of Israel
Movement of which I had been appointed Superintendent. The Jews also heard him gladly. It
was then decided that we start a monthly magazine
in English to acquaint God's people with the
work among the Jews, and at the same time
give through the pages of the magazine the
much needed teachings in the prophetic Word.
I first thought that *The Hope of Israel*, the name
of the Jewish Monthly I was editing, should
be the name of the new monthly. But finally
we decided to call it *Our Hope*. The first issue
was dated July, 1894. It was a small leaflet
of twenty-four pages. We printed not quite
five hundred copies which were carried by one

man to the Post Office. The subscription list was started with personal friends, and as the subscriptions were insufficient to meet the printing costs, some of these friends helped financially. Among these were John S. Huyler, then famous for his good candies; Mr. and Mrs. S. P. Harbison of Pittsburgh, Pa.; Eugen Mosimann, and numerous German believers. Dr. James H. Brookes again came to our help by endorsing the new magazine, urging the readers of *The Truth* to subscribe for it, and a few months later he presented us with his complete mail list, which brought us many new subscribers.

Still it was a hard struggle to keep the magazine going. Many times the regular issues were delayed because there were no funds to meet the bills and the postage. It was suggested that we solicit advertisements and meet the deficiency in this way. I objected to this at once and adhered to this decision. In all the thirty-six years of its publication *Our Hope* has steered clear of commercial advertising and the Lord has graciously sustained me in this course, though often it was hard to make ends meet.

Three years later Dr. James H. Brookes was called away to be with the Lord, whom he had served so well. His magazine was sold and a combination made with Dr. Gordon's magazine *The Watchword.* But *Watchword and Truth* did not continue in the prophetic witness of Drs. Brookes and Gordon, and so it came that *Our Hope* was looked upon as the true and legitimate successor of *The Truth* with the result that hundreds of the old *Truth* readers became readers and supporters of *Our Hope*.

With the publication of the magazine, many calls came from different cities both to Dr. Stroeter and me to hold meetings in behalf of the work for Israel. Both of us preached in English and in German, so that we had a large field before us. Ever since I had begun my Yiddish and Hebrew publications I invited Christians to send for tracts, papers and New Testaments to give out in different localities to help the Jews find the truth. The requests came from over a hundred cities and towns, and great good was done. Many of these places where the friends of Israel circulated these tracts urged meetings for Bible study, especially on prophetic lines and many calls reached us.

Several places in New England were regularly visited: Brockton, Mass.; Lawrence, Lowell and Boston. Dr. Niles in Boston was carrying on a testimony to the Jews, and I spoke for several months to good audiences of Jews in a rented hall. A work was started in Philadelphia and an empty store rented, and for several months we maintained this testimony to the Jews of Philadelphia, holding at the same time meetings with Christian believers for Bible Study. One excellent

Jewish believer started a work in Baltimore under my supervision, and here also for months I was able to give the Gospel to the Jews and interest Gentile believers in the prophetic Word.

In Harrisburg, Pa. a few days Bible Conference had been arranged by George C. Needham, the well-known Evangelist. Some of the Niagara Conference brethren were there, and I addressed a large audience in one of the Lutheran Churches. Then came a call from Altoona, Pa. The First Presbyterian Church opened its doors on a Lord's day, and a great audience gathered to hear my address on "The Future of the Jewish People in the Light of the Bible." The pastor, Dr. B., while the congregation was singing the second hymn before the sermon, turned to me and said: "Now you understand that you will preach about the future of the Jews, and whatever you say, do not mention that second coming business." Inasmuch as the whole Jewish Question is linked with the Messianic question, and no Jewish future is possible apart from the return of our Lord, my whole address was built around this truth. What else could I do but speak out? So I disregarded the old gentleman's request, and gave my testimony with much liberty and power. When I sat down, he got up and expressed his grief that this great audience had been obliged to listen to a premillennial argument, which, he said, was all unscriptural. He tried to answer

my simple arguments from Scripture, and the
more he tried the more he muddled himself up
till finally he did not know himself where he
stood. When the meeting was over several of
his elders came to me and thanked me heartily
for the address and one said: "We have longed
for years for a man to come and to say in this
pulpit what you have said tonight."

I must mention Scranton, Pa. George L. Alrich, in the early nineties, was pastor of the Grace
Reformed Episcopal Church, succeeding Dr. D. M.
Stearns. Mr. Alrich had heard of the New York
work among the Jews, and he invited me to come
and tell his congregation about it. That invitation brought great results. For more than
five years I held meetings in this church, and
while Mr. Alrich was an earnest Christian, he
had but little knowledge of prophecy and other
truths. He was a sweet-spirited brother, humble
and teachable. These visits of mine were a
great help and blessing to him. A number of
years later he left the regular ministry and went
out in Bible teaching work, and brought great
help to hundreds of people.

While this enlarged testimony was going on,
the work in New York City continued with
the same large meetings. A number of Jews
confessed Christ. Joseph Rabinowitz of Russia
had been asked by M r. D. L. Moody to come to
Chicago. He responded and I met him in New

York on his way back to Russia. He was a remarkable man. A prosperous lawyer in Kishineff, where I visited him in 1895, he had had an interesting experience, when his co-religionists sent him to Palestine to start there a colony for Russian Jews. By reading a Hebrew New Testament He found Jesus of Nazareth to be Israel's true Messiah. Professor Franz Delitzsch of Leipzig baptised him, and the great scholar, a strong believer in Israel's future restoration, said on his conversion, "The first ripe fig from the barren fig tree has fallen." I invited him to speak to a large gathering of Jews in Rivington Street. He was a great Hebrew scholar and his heart was deeply stirred when he faced so large an audience. After his return I received the following communication from him:

Pastor A. C. Gaebelein,

My beloved Brother in the Lord:

Your affectionate letter was duly received, and I am delighted to read in the same that peace and life is with you, and that God helps you to build up the house of Israel. I praise Him that He gives you strength to gather out a few of His chosen people in America, and I am glad to hear everywhere of the name you have among my people. I am likewise glad to hear that my presence with you in New York is still fresh in your memory. I think that the greetings I sent you recently will show you how much I honor you, and how dear your work is to me.

Be strong and of good courage; keep silent to all attacks of false brethren. Israel shall yet be honored. I am well aware of the greatness of your work and trouble for the good of Israel. Since the Lord showed me the state of my brethren in your land my soul is very anxious to know what is being done there. For you, beloved brother my prayer is to the living God, that the door which has been opened to you shall never be closed by such men who say, We are Jews.

He will not forsake you in your glorious work, but strengthen you till our Messiah arrives in glory and majesty.

I love and honor you.

Your brother in Jesus Christ,

Joseph Rabinowitz.

The preaching of the Gospel which continued weekly without any intermission brought fruit. A nice company of believers from Israel had been gathered and we held weekly a special service with them for prayer and Bible instruction. In looking over our reports I find the record of a meeting held in January 1895 when we gathered around the Lord's table to remember Him. Twenty-three Hebrew believers were present and several who remembered the Lord for the first time were greatly moved. The same month we ventured a Jewish service in English. I invited Dr. William J. Erdman to speak to about five hundred Hebrews. A number of English-speaking friends were present, among them Mr. Malachi Taylor, Dr. Van Alstine and Mr. Niedringhaus of St. Louis. Dr. Erdman spoke and I translated sentence after sentence. His text was "The Just Shall Live by Faith."

He asked the Hebrew audience, "Was Abraham living before the law was given or after the law?" Some answered from the audience, "He lived before the law." Then said Dr. Erdman, "He certainly could not be just by the works of the law, because there was no law. But the Bible states that Abraham believed God and it was counted to him for righteousness. Don't you Jews want to be saved in the same way as your father Abraham was saved?" They certainly listened most attentively to this address.

But the difficulty was that these Jewish friends who attended regularly and those who believed were a wandering lot. Many were young men and found better employment elsewhere, so that we missed many from our gatherings. But they wrote us letters and kept in touch with the work. Here is a specimen letter dated Providence, R. I.

Dear Friend and Brother in Jesus:

I am now safely here in Providence and have found work already. But if I would follow the feeling of my heart I would take the next boat back to New York. I feel strange here among my Jewish brethren. I miss the services in Rivington Street so much. Oh, may the Lord help me to be faithful, and do especially what you have said, to speak everywhere about the Lord our Messiah. I live now in 20 Summer Street, and as you promised, please send me the *Tiqweth Israel* (the Yiddish Monthly) regularly. My greetings to the brethren.

Your faithful disciple,

L. M.

After a few months most of the believing Jews had moved to other cities; years later I met some of them in Western States. This reminds me of a novel experience in connection with the Stony Brook School. Several years ago a bright boy attended the school and graduated with great honors. His father is a Methodist preacher, a Hebrew Christian. He told me when we met that over thirty years ago when a youngster he came frequently to Rivington Street to hear me preach and that the Word made a deep impression upon him. So who knows what fruit this witness-bearing has brought? There is a day coming when it will be fully known.

From the very start of my work among the Jewish people, I felt that they should not be Gentilized and that the attempt to make Methodists, Baptists, Lutherans or Presbyterians out of them would be a mistake. Dr. Stroeter fully shared this viewpoint with me and we formulated the Hope of Israel Principles. Our conception was that a believing Hebrew should not sever his connection with the nation, but though a believer in our Lord as Israel's true Messiah, he should not separate himself from his brethren. Mr. Bowles Colgate of Colgate & Co., New York, expressed our principles in an article in the *N. Y. Christian Advocate* which I quote.

Mr. Gaebelein fully shares the belief of orthodox Jews in the fulfillment of prophecy and the restoration of Israel to the promised land, and his method of work is not to antagonize the Jewish customs, or to deprive converts of their hold and influence with their own people, by making Gentiles of them, but to induce them to become real Hebrew-Christians, accepting Christ as the Messiah, but continuing to observe their own laws and customs, as far as they do not conflict with the essentials of the Christian faith.

These principles were abandoned by me several years later when I understood more fully the revealed truth as to the church, the body of Christ. In that body there is neither Jew nor Gentile; all are one in Christ. So long as this body is forming the believing Jew is added by the Spirit of God as a member to the body of Christ. It will be far different after the body of Christ, the true Church is completed. There will then be called a remnant, God-fearing, Bible-believing, and Messiah-expecting, from the people Israel. They will continue in connection with the unbelieving nation and bear a witness to the coming King, whom they know is our Lord Jesus Christ. It is this believing remnant of the future which will receive the promises.

A fine young Hebrew had accepted Christ and I had baptized him. He felt called to go back to Poland to witness to his brethren there. Paul Rosenzweig left in 1894 to carry on work in a small Polish village where he had to suffer a great deal of persecution. Later he laboured for several years in Warsaw with good success.

Another assistant I had was Harry Zackhausen. He was a Russian Jew, and earnest believer in Christ, and he attended Dr. Dowkont's Medical Missionary Institute. He visited frequently other cities where he spoke to the Jews. Mr. Mark Levy, an English Hebrew of excellent character, who had suffered much on account of having confessed Christ, also worked with us. He visited Scranton, Pa. and other places and spent some time in Atlanta, Georgia. I pass over numerous other assistants who labored under my direction in Philadelphia, Baltimore, and elsewhere. The work in Rosenhayn, N. J., already mentioned, progressed well and Miss Snow did an excellent work there.

The circulation of Hebrew, Yiddish, English, and German literature increased constantly. In 1895 the first editions of *Joseph and His Brethren* were printed in Yiddish and found hundreds of eager readers, while the *Tiqweth Israel*, our Yiddish monthly, appeared in very much enlarged editions, and thousands were sent to many other States and to different European countries.

CHAPTER V

EVER since I had produced Jewish-Christian literature, and especially since the publication of the *Hope of Israel* in Yiddish, I received letters from Russia and other Eastern European countries. Some of these letters showed a real soul-hunger and a great desire for more literature was expressed. Many Jews in New York suggested that I should make a trip to Russia to get first-hand information as to Jewish conditions. I had a great desire to go and to bear witness in that land and wherever the Lord might open a door.

In the early summer of 1895 our prayers were answered, and a friend of the work gave sufficient money to start me on the trip across the ocean and to undertake an extended trip into the great Russian Empire. Through the influence of another friend I obtained from the Secretary of State in Washington a letter of introduction to our ambassador in St. Petersburg (at that time the Hon. Mr. Breckenridge) and to the different consular offices. I left New York in August, and after a brief visit to my home in Germany to spend a few days with my parents, I took the train for Poland.

The trip from start to finish was marked by the most extraordinary providential leadings. It was a great undertaking, but I knew it was the Lord's call and that He would be my keeper in all my ways. I carried with me only the most necessary things, so as not to be hindered in traveling. But I also had a heavy box filled with my Yiddish tracts and some Russian Gospel literature. Now at that time there was a very strict censorship in force. To carry a large amount of Christian Evangelical literature into Russia was forbidden. The Stundist movement had drawn the fire of the Holy Synod of Russia and hundreds were being banished and had to suffer severely for Christ's sake. My heart beat faster and faster the nearer we came to the Russian-Polish border. Finally the train stopped and a heavily armed Russian officer demanded my passport and I had to leave the carriage with my belongings. "Ah," he said, "You are from America." He spoke in German and engaged me in a friendly conversation. He wanted a lot of information about our country and why I had come over there, what I intended to do, how long I would stay. Then he pointed to my large suitcase and the box filled with tracts. I told him that these were my personal belongings, and he kindly answered: "I am not going to trouble you unpacking everything; I shall just look into one of the two." Then he selected my suitcase and looked through it, and the box with the literature was not opened and escaped confiscation. As my passport was all right, I shook hands with the officer and we proceeded towards my first stopping place—Lodz in Poland.

I arrived on Saturday. I went to a synagogue, I believe the largest in that city, mingled with the Jews, engaged them in conversation, and as I wore at that time a full beard, they took me for a Jew. Then I called on the pastor of a large Lutheran Church where, I had prayed, I might have an opportunity to preach the Gospel on my first Lord's day in Poland. The pastor was away on his vacation and my hope to preach faded away. I went back to my hotel and took a place at a table in the dining room, asking the waiter to bring me the "Speise-karte," the menu. He evidently misunderstood me and brought me the directory of Lodz. I opened it at random, and the first name I saw was the name of Pastor G. of the German Baptist Church. After a hasty supper I set out to find him. He was at home and when I mentioned my name he said he had heard of my work and gave me a most hearty welcome. His church building was very large. I preached to a splendid congregation in the morning. Then an afternoon service was held, and as it was noised about that a preacher from America would preach, we had an immense crowd, among them not a few Jews. I continued for several days with increasing audiences. Great good was done in these first meetings I was privileged to hold on this trip. It was also an encouragement when a good brother handed the pastor 50 rubels (twenty-five dollars) to help in my journey. During that week I had interesting conversations with Jews. It would fill too many pages if I recorded my visits to Warsaw and Wilna.

I was unknown in St. Petersburg. After calling on our ambassador, Mr. Breckenridge, who received me very kindly, and on General von Wahl, the Police Commissioner of the city, an excellent Christian, I strolled through the streets, and turning into a side alley I noticed a small bookstore in which German Bibles and tracts were displayed. I entered and found a dear brother in charge. I introduced myself, and he answered, "You know I read about your coming to Russia and I have prayed ever since that the Lord might guide you here, and now He has answered my prayers. Oh, how happy I am that you have come." He closed his shop to visit all the Christian friends he knew to arrange for a meeting that very evening in a private house. A goodly number had gathered. There was a simple meal with the ever-present Russian "Samovar" for preparation of hot tea on the table, and I was asked to speak. That was around eight in the evening. The meeting lasted long till after midnight. I closed it at least five times, but each time some one spoke up and said, "Oh! give us some more."

A number of meetings were held by me; in one I spoke through an interpreter. It was a secret meeting. I also received a courteous invitation from Baron Nicolai to be his guest in his summer estate in Wiborg, Finland. "Mon Repos", as the place was called, was a charming spot. His mother, Baroness Nicolai, was a very godly woman. Several others came to the Bible readings I gave, among them Count and Countess Shuwalov. The days I spent with them were very happy. And there were many others of the Russian nobility who were earnest believers and loved the Word of God. I mention Princesse Lieven and Princesse Gagarin. They became deeply interested readers of *Our Hope*, and circulated not a few of my books. I also had the privilege of addressing a good meeting in Wiborg. One of the attendants was the Count of Griepenberg and his family, who later during the Russo-Japanese war, led one of the Russian armies.

I must pass over my visits to Moscow, Minsk, and other places. In Kieff I had a blessed time meeting numerous Jews, among them several earnest believers. I held one secret meeting with them. Here I met Professor S., who had charge of the prosecution of the Stundists. Brother Wolobruski, a Hebrew believer, acted as interpreter. The interview took several hours. He wanted to know what I preached, what I believed, if I had brought any money with me to give away, or if I intended to start a new church. When he heard that my only aim was to preach Christ, that I would never say a word against the Greek Orthodox Church and would never mix in politics, he declared himself willing to obtain for me the permission of the Governor of the Province, Count Ignateff, to go anywhere to preach.

One close escape I must record. During my visit in Russia there were thousands of cases of Asiatic cholera with great fatalities. The censorship suppressed the real conditions, but there were placards everywhere telling the people not to drink water, but to have it boiled, etc. I was ignorant of the state of things. One noon I was suddenly seized with all the symptoms of this awful scourge. My medical knowledge suggested at once what to do. I was alone and after calling on Him and reminding Him of my childhood verse, "Call upon Me in the day of trouble, and I will deliver thee," I sent for the remedies I needed and in a short time a reaction set in; my prayer was answered, the means used— repeated doses of spirits of camphor—had been blessed, and I recovered rapidly but suffered from much weakness.

Then followed a happy meeting with dear brother Rabinowitz in Kishineff in Bessarabia. He met me, embraced me, kissed me, and gave thanks in Hebrew that I had come. I had hardly been fifteen minutes in the hotel room to change my clothes, when an elegant carriage drove up and a gentleman called on me. Baron von Stachelberg brought a most gracious invitation from his wife, the Baroness, to be guest of honour at a dinner on the following day. It was a splendid affair. I met many of the leading people of Kishineff among them the venerable Pastor Faltin, for many years pastor of the Lutheran Church. Our fellowship was sweet. But the fellowship with Rabinowitz was the best of all. I attended his Hebrew-Christian Synagogue. I spoke to his congregation. We took sweet council together. He longed for a godly remnant in the midst of the ungodly nation. He toiled for this and hoped to see it accomplished. A few years later the Lord called him home.

I cannot describe our farewell. We prayed together. Then he kissed me again and again, and said in Hebrew: "Jehovah bless thee and keep thee! Peace upon thy path; peace in thy heart; peace upon thy house; Shulom aleichem! Shulom aleichem!" He handed me a little Hebrew New Testament in which he had written a verse in Hebrew. A year later I received from him an illuminating treatise on the Person of our Lord, which I had printed in 25,000 copies. It must have helped hundreds of Jews.

I pass by my experiences in Roumania, in Czernowitz, Satagura and Stanislaus. I made a

second visit to Poland and took brother Rosenzweig from a miserable Polish village to Warsaw,
his future field of labour. How glad I would
have been to remain longer, but it was quite
necessary for me to return to the work in New
York. The Lord brought me safely back home
to my loved ones and to my work.

On my return I found that our Hebrew friends
were greatly interested in the trip abroad. They
had heard of it through different sources. Saturday after Saturday the same large audiences
gathered to listen to the preaching of the Word
of God. I find among my records the following:
Last Saturday morning (First Saturday in December, 1895) I preached on Jonah, a type of the
Messiah and the Jewish nation. I quoted in
my discourse Hosea vi:2: "After two days He
will revive us, on the third day He will raise
us up, and we shall live in His sight." I mentioned
that the first day during which Israel was dead
nationally was the Babylonian captivity; the
second day means the dispersion of the nation
during this age. Then I gave a description of
the third day, when like Jonah, taken out of his
grave, Israel will be restored and live in His
sight. I closed this discourse with an exhortation
to accept Him now as individuals and not wait
for that national hope, that each Jew needs a
Saviour from sin, and Christ is the only Saviour.

A few days later an orthodox Jew visited me.

He had been in the meeting and brought a piece of paper on which he had written the comments of leading Jewish rabbis on Hosea vi. He had extracts from Kimchi, Rashi, the Yalkutim, etc. and he said, "They all say what you preached last Sabbath morning."

Inasmuch as the demand for Yiddish and Hebrew literature had greatly increased since my trip to Russia, we had to issue almost monthly 5,000 copies of the Yiddish magazine. Paul Rosenzweig sent most encouraging reports from Warsaw and urged us to send big supplies, and similar requests came from scores of other places in Eastern Europe, not to speak of the many Gentile friends in the United States who received regularly copies to distribute among their Jewish neighbors. An enormous quantity of literature was sent forth during the winter of 1895-96. At the same time requests came from many different churches in Eastern and Central states to come and speak on the Jews, the Return of our Lord, and to hold a few meetings with the Jews in these different places and give them the Gospel.

I must mention again the fact that the New York City Mission only furnished the buildings and provided for a monthly allowance for myself. But we needed many thousands of dollars for the publications, assistants, relief of the poor, etc. And thus I was cast on the Lord to supply these needs. How graciously He answered prayer! Several times it seemed as if I would have to stop, but when the need was the greatest prayer was answered and all needs were again supplied.

There is a special mention made in my records of the services held by me during the Passover feast of the Jews.

"The feast of Pesach (Passover) has been appropriately observed by us. I preached several discourses on the significance of Passover and on Him who is the true Passover Lamb. Extensive preparations were made by orthodox Jews for weeks ahead for this feast of rejoicing. Conscientiously the houses were cleaned up, and every morsel which might contain 'chometz' (leaven) was thrown away. Literally the old leaven was purged out, witnessed to by heaps of refuse on the sidewalks. Then wagons loaded with 'Matzoth' (unleavened bread) passed through the streets. At last the festive evening arrived. Like magic the busy scenes were hushed after sun-down and the candles were lit. Families could be seen in every story of the large tenements gathering around the 'festive table' on which were three unleavened cakes, a meat bone and bitter herbs, and then the impressive service, the Hagada, was read. One extra glass of wine stands on the table; it is for Elijah the prophet, the fore-runner of the long expected Messiah. The old, long-bearded Jew says again as he has said so many times, sometimes choked with tears, 'This year here—next year in Jerusalem?' What a wonderful feast it is! What a witness to the truth of God's everlasting Word, vouchsafing that still greater, coming deliverance, when the Lord brings them back from all countries!"

Large gatherings had been attending, and on one afternoon we had stirring times. As long as I spoke on the historical Passover the greatest attention and quietness reigned. But as soon as I mentioned that Passover when Christ appeared and when He died as the Lamb of God, an orthodox Jew, who had watched me closely, got up and left. I continued, when suddenly another one got up, protested in Yiddish like a rapid-firing gun, and left. Then followed a great uproar. They cried, "Come out! Come out! Don't listen to an uncircumcised Gentile. Jesus is not our Messiah!" Others in the audiences shouted to them "Sit down!" One of the most appalling experiences was when young Jewish children came, asked for a paper or a tract to hand to their parents, and as soon as they had received it they would howl with delight and shriek out some of the most awful insults to our Lord, while they tore up the papers and stamped on them. Such is the blindness of the people, who are, nevertheless, beloved for the Father's sake. April, 1896 was marked by the publication of new Gospel literature for the Jews. One was a tract on *Prayer* and the other on *The Third Day*. They were printed in editions of 8,000 and the same month we issued a tract on *True Peace* printed in Judeo-Spanish for free circulation through missionaries in North Africa.

During May, 1896, Professor Stroeter left New York to go to Europe. *Our Hope*—Vol. II, page 241 contains this note: "On May, 27 Mr. Stroeter expects to sail for Europe, to be gone about three months. Many invitations to speak which Mr. Gaebelein received last year, could not be accepted for want of time. Another and not least object in making this trip is a visit to Warsaw, where our dear brother Rosenzweig is laboring so faithfully. We desire to strengthen the hands and cheer the heart of our dear brother, who meets with much opposition and discouragement, as much as lies in us."

Dr. Stroeter found open doors everywhere. I must give an extract from his letter written in Lodz, where a year before I had given my first testimony in Poland.

"I am here in Lodz at the home of Pastor G. Brother Rosenzweig is sitting in an armchair nearby reading, while I am writing to you. He sends his love to you. He followed me here this morning on an early train. I came last night from Warsaw. This morning I stood in the same narrow and high pulpit where you preached a year ago to this congregation. The Lord gave

me great liberty. This evening I shall preach
again, also tomorrow. During the day we visit
Jews. What a harvest field there is in Poland!
Would that we could have a hundred Rosenzweigs
here. Yesterday afternoon there came to this
house some fifteen or sixteen earnest and inquiring
men, some white with age, others young; some
hearty believers in Christ and others inquiring.
There was an excellent spirit prevailing. God is
using our brother greatly."

Dr. Stroeter made several trips to Europe and
finally settled there permanently with his family.
He continued to do an excellent work among
Jews and Gentiles, also editing a German paper,
till the Lord called him home.

The summer of 1896 was very trying. Some
of the assistants dropped out, and I had to do most
of the work. I had hoped to visit camp meetings,
summer conventions, but I had to keep on toiling
in our East Side Ghetto. In spite of temperatures
of 90 to 95 the people continued to come. There
were many evidences of His blessing and that
was the real refreshment for me.

Then came again the Jewish holidays early in
September. Volume III of *Our Hope* page 106
has this interesting account: "We held three
services during the Rosh-Hashonoh (New Year),
September 8 and 9. The service on the eve of
New Year was not largely attended, but the
other services brought great audiences. The

story of Isaac's birth and the intended sacrifice on Moriah was being read in the synagogues. I read the same lessons. I took as a text a sentence from the Jewish orthodox prayer book— 'Look upon the Lamb of Morijah' meaning, of course, the substitute ram which Abraham offered instead of Isaac. I spoke of the true Lamb, our gracious substitute. There was a remarkable attention and many were visibly moved. Mr. Jospe, a Hebrew believer of many years, followed in a brief address."

In November of 1896 the publication of *Our Hope* was delayed because there were no funds, but prayer was again answered, so that we could issue a double number.

This brings us to the year 1897, which was marked by some very important events. In the first place I notified the City Mission of the Methodist denomination that I would no longer receive the monthly allowance, but trust the Lord for my support. This led to the work becoming interdenominational, or rather, un-denominational. We made the following public announcement:

"The authorities of that denomination to whom the Superintendent and Secretary of the Hope of Israel Movement have been responsible, not only personally, but administratively, have now, upon our own request, without assuming any further responsibilities, allowed us to continue on interdenominational lines. The movement is therefore no longer under the supervision of the City Mission Society. It seems likewise, that in the providence of God, the time has come for a change of locality for the varied work (evangelistic, literary, charitable) of the Hope of Israel." This was the first step made by me towards my larger work from coast to coast. All was under His gracious guidance, though His purpose as to my future ministry was then unknown to me. Inasmuch as No. 209 Madison Street had been sold, we rented quarters at 128 Second Street, from where we sent out our literature and had our meetings with Hebrew believers and inquirers. The Saturday and Sunday meetings continued at the Allen Street Memorial, No. 91 Rivington Street. We then began to pay rent for the use of the building. The work continued under the same blessing. Here is a paragraph speaking of this: "Our meetings continue to be very well attended. A few Saturdays ago I noticed a Hebrew in the audience whom I had not seen for four years. He was one of the first who had found a better life in trusting in Christ, having been an infidel and anarchist. He had traveled much, and coming again to the city he paid us a visit at once. If all those who accepted Christ during our five years ministry among the Jews in down-town New York were with us today, we would have, no doubt, a strong and interesting congregation."

More and more calls came from the outside for Bible teaching meetings, especially on prophetic lines. Besides my regular visits to Pittsburg, Philadelphia, Pa., Lawrence and Boston, Mass, where I met this year (1897) for the first time James M. Gray, pastor of a Reformed Episcopal Church, I also visited regularly St. Louis, Mo. This was brought about through a consecrated Christian woman, Mrs. Clara D. Ely, who had a great love for the Gospel and also for Israel. She rented an old church building on Morgan Street, Corner of 19th Street, and for some time I made monthly visits there gathering in the Jews and also having Bible Conferences with Christian believers. We had many great blessings there. Other places visited for the first time were Toronto, Ontario; Chattanooga, Tennessee, and Atlanta, Georgia; St. Paul and Minneapolis, Minn.

The work abroad increased. Many new doors were opened for Dr. Stroeter and a testimony was also started in Palestine. Brother Rosenzweig continued in his work and reached out after many new places. How effectual his testimony was is learned from the many communications I received from Poland.

It would be impossible to follow the work done in New York and elsewhere during 1897-98. The blessing through the printed page became more and more evident. The treatise on the

Life and Work of our Lord, written by Joseph Rabinowitz, and published in an edition of 25,000 resulted in great blessing. During the first three months of 1898, besides regular monthly visits to St. Louis, I held meetings in Peoria, Illinois; Kansas City and Carrolton, Mo.; in Wilkes-Barre, Pa.; and in several New England towns.

In May, 1898 our first prophetic conference was held in Berkeley Temple, Boston, Mass. The speakers besides me were: W. J. Erdman, J. M. Gray, Frank Weston and Professor Chapell. This was followed by a conference in Brockton, Mass. During this summer I was one of the speakers at the Niagara Bible Conference, which was held at Point Chautauqua, Lake Chautauqua, N. Y. The speakers were: Professor W. G. Morehead, Major Whittle, C. I. Scofield, J. B. Parsons, Elmore Harris, L. W. Munhall and myself. I delivered three addresses on "The Song of Moses," "The Parables of Balaam," and "The Ode of Habbakuk." Dear Dr. Brookes was much missed. But here I met for the first time a beloved brother and his good wife, Mr. and Mrs. Francis Emory Fitch, who became later such a help in my ministry.

Dr. Stroeter had left on his third trip to Europe, so that I was left alone with the work again. The Lord supplied energy and strength and all spiritual need to continue in it. In reading over the issues of *Our Hope* in which the work and the various activities are recorded month after month, I can but thank God for His kindness and mercy in permitting me to do this work. It was all done to spread His truth and to help Jews and Gentiles. Some day I shall find in His own glorious presence the harvest from the seed sown.

A second great conference was held in Dr. Brookes's old church in St. Louis, Mo., December 4-7. The speakers were: R. A. Torrey, W. J. Erdman, H. M. Parsons, Professor W. G. Morehead, and A. C. Gaebelein. This conference was preceded by one held in Dayton, Ohio; Professor Morehead and I were the two speakers.

PART III

THE NEW COMMISSION

CHAPTER VI

THE YEAR 1899 brought a great change under the guidance of Him whom I served. My interest in the Jewish people had begun almost eight years before. As the reader has learned, the testimony to Israel was greatly blessed and owned of the Lord. Thousands upon thousands heard the Gospel preached. The circulation of Gospel literature had become phenomenal. A Yiddish Monthly found many thousands of readers, and tons of tracts, most of them written by me, were circulated in a number of languages. One of these tracts was published in Mahrati for the so-called black Jews in India; another was printed in Judeo-Spanish and distributed in North Africa. Mr. Simon Bauer worked in Palestine; Abraham Kestin circulated our Arabic tracts in Egypt and Paul Rosenzweig had worked several years in Poland. This work had been started in connection with the City Mission Society of the Methodist Episcopal Church. It soon became evident, as stated before, that this work could not be confined to a single denomination. Gradually the work had become interdenominational. We had formulated the Hope of Israel Principles. In these principles we stated the following: "The Jew has no need whatever of the organizations and institutions of historical (i. e. Gentile and denominational) Christianity. All he needs is personal, saving faith in His own Jewish Messiah, the Christ of God, nothing more." *I still believe this great principle.* What these principles declared, that the believing Jew in Christ does not cease to be a Jew and should continue as under the law, I had also taught, for a time at least. New light had come to me from the Scriptures. While I had found in the Bible the great truths concerning Israel's future regeneration and national restoration and believed with all my heart in "that blessed hope," His promised return and the kindred truths, the truth concerning the true church, the body and bride of Christ, as revealed in the Epistle to the Ephesians and in the Epistle to the Colossians had only recently dawned upon me.

I was therefore forced to give up these principles, while my associate, Dr. Stroeter refused to give them up. This led to our separation, which had become necessary because he wished to settle in Europe. In September 1899 in a lengthy document, printed in *Our Hope*, I said:

"The principles which teach that a Jew who has believed in Christ and is therefore a member of His body, the church, should or may continue as under the law, practice circumcision, keep the seventh day (Saturday), eat only clean food as commanded by Moses and keep the different feasts, the writer does no longer believe to be scriptural. The great revelations of the Lord in the Church Epistles concerning His body are entirely ignored in these principles. The following passages make it very clear that these ordinances are no longer binding or even existing for a believer in Christ, be he Jew or Gentile.

"He is our peace, who hath made both one, and brake down the middle wall of partition, having abolished in His flesh the enmity, even the law of commandments contained in ordinances; that He might create in Himself of the twain one new man, so making peace; and might reconcile them both in one body unto God through the Cross, having slain the enmity thereby, and He came and preached peace to you that were afar off and peace to them that were nigh" (Ephes. ii:14-18). "Let no man therefore judge you in meat, or in drink, or in respect of a feast day, or a new moon, or a Sabbath day, which are a shadow of things to come, but the body is Christ's" (Col. ii:16-17). "Ye have put on the new man, which is being renewed unto the knowledge after the image of Him that created Him, where there cannot be (literal rendering) Greek or Jew, circumcision and uncircumcision, barbarian, Scythian, bondman, freeman; but Christ is all and in all" (Col. iii:10, 11).

At the same time I passed through deep soul exercise as to my own position. I had learned from Scripture that there is but one church; not different bodies, but one body. The prayer of our Lord "that they may be one, as we are" (John xvii:11) had been answered on the day of Pentecost with the coming of God the Holy Spirit. The assembled believers were then baptized by the Spirit into one body and ever since all true believers are united by the same Spirit to that one body. "For by one Spirit are we all baptised into one body, whether we be Jews or Gentiles, whether we be bond or free; and have been all made to drink into one Spirit" (1 Cor. xii:13). This great truth came to my heart as one of the greatest of all revelations. As I entered into a deeper study of that matchless document, the Ephesian Epistle, containing the highest revelation, that mystery which was hidden in God in former ages, the truth concerning the church, as the body of Christ, became not only most precious to me, but it demanded practical expression in my life. We are exhorted to give all diligence to keep the unity of the Spirit in the bond of peace (Ephes. iv:3), but denominationalism is a practical denial of that unity. The sad divisions as they exist in Protestantism appeared to me not as the work of the Spirit, but as the work of the flesh, even as the New Testament teaches.

Then I meditated much on the ministry in that body. The Lord to whom I had yielded

my young life in 1879 to be His servant had graciously given me gifts for the ministry. I was
entrusted with it "for the perfecting of the saints
unto the work of the ministry, for the edifying
of the body of Christ" (Ephes. iv:12). Then it
gradually came to me that my future ministry
whether to Jews or Gentiles, believers in Christ,
must be exercised according to this truth. The
new commission came to me in the early part of
1899 to go forth denominationally unaffiliated,
to minister to the body of Christ, wherever it
is found and wherever my Lord would open the
door.

For several years the beloved brethren of the
Niagara testimony had spoken of the great need
of a nation-wide effort to disseminate especially
prophetic truths. I had heard Drs. Erdman,
Morehead, Marvin, Stifler and others speak of
what ought to be done, but it never came to a
realization of such an ideal effort. Afresh I
dedicated my life to Him, who led me forth by a
renewed commission into this larger field.

Then something happened in the providence
of the Lord, which helped me to sever my connection with the Methodist Episcopal denomination, and which made it possible to go forth in the
larger ministry in His Name. I find in the
April issue of *Our Hope* in the year 1899 the
following editorial note:

"In a New York meeting of evangelical minis-ters the following statements were made and the day after heralded throughout the country:

> The absolutely inerrancy and infallibility of the Bible are no longer possible of belief among reasoning men. . . . Half the pages of the Old Tesment are of unknown authorship, and the New Testament contains contradictions.

"This is called 'higher criticism'! How much harm this higher nonsense is doing throughout our land no one can estimate."

The meeting mentioned was the weekly Methodist preachers' meeting held in the Methodist Book Concern. I was present and listened to the address given by the now nationally famous radio speaker, Dr. S. P. Cadman. He was at that time pastor of the Central Methodist Church. In that address the Mosaic authorship of the Pentateuch was denied. The historicity of the Book of Jonah and other Scriptures was attacked. Yet here were several hundred Methodist preachers applauding the remarks which were but a faint echo of German rationalism. When I protested and suggested that charges should be brought against a man who uttered such unwarranted attacks upon the Book of books, I was told by high officials not to be hasty about this, "for," as one said, "sooner or later we must fall in line with these results of scholarly Bible Criticism." When I heard this, I decided at once to sever my fellowship with the denomination, and though different inducements were offered me, if I would change my mind, the Lord gave courage to carry out my decision and I withdrew to follow, as a servant, Him who has promised the open door to those who keep His Word and who do not deny His Name.

While all this was done after much prayer, I spoke to different brethren about it, as well as about my future ministry. One of the brethren, Dr. L. W. Munhall, advised me to stay right in the Methodist Church and, to quote his own words, "fight them as hard as you can." Our brother has done this himself for more than fifty years, but it seems that he has not succeeded very well. Dr. W. J. Erdman warned against it. He said "It cannot be done in this country. You will not have any calls to service," he said, "when people find out that you are an independent." I still hear him say, "Gaebelein, your history will be written in about two years." I answered: "My brother, does service depend on the backing of an ecclesiastical organization or on the Lord in Glory and the Holy Spirit? That is the question. I believe the Lord is able to take care of me."

E. P. Marvin declared, "Well, brother, if the apostasy continues in the different denominations, we all must take the same step sooner or later. The Lord bless you." Equally encouraging were the words of Dr. C. I. Scofield and other brethren. The step was done in faith and I was facing much opposition and many difficulties. Many times my little-big verse was used, and it became more and more real: "Call upon Me in the day of trouble: I will deliver thee, and thou shalt glorify Me." The many answered prayers, providential leadings, and increasing spiritual blessings were the gracious seals of His approval. One thing after the other proved that He was leading in the gradual realization of the vision.

What about the testimony to Israel? I gave up the office quarters at 128 Second Street and moved to the next block and established offices, a book depository and a reading room at No. 80. I continued to rent the Allen Street Memorial Church, where I had ministered for eight years, and the attendance continued good and encouraging. A short time after, the Methodist Board decided to put this church-building in the market. It was sold later and became a synagogue. It was difficult to find a suitable place in the Ghetto. There were large halls, but the owners were Jews and they refused to hire their halls to a Christian minister. It became evident that in the Jewish quarter the door for ministry was closed. For several years I used on Saturdays a German Evangelical Church building in East Houston Street, but as it was some distance from the Jewish quarter the attendance decreased, though the blessing through the ministry of the Gospel to

the Jews continued. The distribution of literature was kept up over five years longer.

I was convinced that the work had been done,
and that the new commission would make it impossible to continue in New York, doing a work
which demanded my continued presence, and
supervision.

As stated in the previous chapter, during the
Niagara Bible Conference held at Point Chautauqua I had met Mr. and Mrs. Francis E. Fitch,
of New York. Mr. Fitch had a printing establishment on Broad Street, New York. I had turned
over to him the printing of *Our Hope*, and as
he was a beloved brother in the Lord I had con-
fided in him as to my vision of ministry and about
my separation from denominationalism. He felt
very happy about it, for he was one of the "Brethren," commonly called "Plymouth Brethren," of
whose existence I knew nothing till I met Mr.
Fitch. Knowing my struggles, he was very generous in his fellowship and helped in many ways.

For many years Mr. Malachi Taylor had held
noonday meetings in Temple Court, an office
building in the financial district of the city. He
was a very able teacher of the Bible. When Mr.
Taylor passed away, Mr. Fitch invited me to go to
the room where Malachi Taylor had conducted
these meetings and to take up this ministry. I did
so several times a week for two years. These noon-
day meetings were conducted in a very simple

way. After prayer a book-study was taken up and continued as long as time permitted. The next day the study was resumed where it was left off the day before. I taught the Gospel of Matthew, the Book of Psalms, the Epistle to the Romans, and other Scriptures. These meetings became a great blessing to me, for as I studied the Word and tried to expound it, the Lord led me deeper and deeper into His Truth. While I tried to water others, I was watered myself. The attendance was not very large, generally from 20 to 30. Here I met John T. Pirie, senior member of the Carson, Pirie & Scott Co. of Chicago and New York, who was a regular attendant; also Frederick K. Day, who is still deeply interested in the work I am doing. A number of young men attended, among them Mr. Hugh R. Monro.

Mr. and Mrs. Fitch carried on a Gospel testimony in Passaic, N. J. For over a year I went there every Lord's day and conducted a Bible reading during the week. Furthermore I met Mr. Alwyn Ball, Jr., another life-long friend, whose fellowship was such a help, and I also conducted weekly Bible readings in his home in Rutherford. All these meetings were most helpful to me, and I was used in helping others. Through these brethren beloved I had become acquainted with the works of those able and godly men who were used in the great spiritual movement of the Brethren in the early part of the nineteenth century, John

Nelson Darby and others. I found in his writings, in the works of William Kelly, McIntosh, F. W. Grant, Bellett and others the soul food I needed. I esteem these men next to the Apostles in their sound and spiritual teaching. But as for an actual affiliation with any of the numerous parties of Brethrenism I could not consent to this, for I found that the party-spirit among these different divisions was even more sectarian than the sectarianism of the larger denominations. Nor did I feel that it was my commission to denounce denominations, as is so often done. Denominationalism exists, and there is nothing that will change it. But my commission was to go and minister the Truth wherever the Lord would open a door for His servant. Invitations to hold Bible Conferences from many States came in increasing numbers, and with the year 1900 began that nationwide ministry, which it has been my privilege to follow for thirty years.

CHAPTER VII

WITH this new departure in my service for the Lord, *Our Hope*, which was started in 1894, led to a new ministry. While in previous years much space was given to the work among the Jews, and information as to Israel was the leading feature, with 1899 the publication became more of a Bible Study magazine, with special emphasis on the prophetic portions of the Scriptures. I began a series of expository articles on the Prophet Zechariah, which appeared every month till the fourteen chapters were covered. As I did this, the subscription list increased. Then I introduced the editorial notes, which are mostly of a devotional character, and for some twenty years the first editorial paragraph has been devoted to something touching the Person, the Glory, and the Work of our ever-blessed Lord. After the exposition of Zechariah was finished, I wrote an exposition of the Gospel of Matthew. This serial Bible teaching is still done in the magazine. At present each issue carries an exposition of a Psalm. I believe this expository teaching has made *Our Hope* so beloved to thousands of believers throughout the English-speaking world. Another department was added and called "Notes on Prophecy and the Jews," and a few years later I

started "Current Events in the Light of the
Bible." This monthly review of current events
made the magazine still more acceptable. Several
leading journalists have complimented me very
highly on it. It was interesting to see when
the great war passed into history, that having followed closely European events, I actually predicted such a European conflagration, not because
I am a prophet or the son of a prophet, but on
account of close observation. The Sunday School
Lessons were furnished with a brief exposition
by Dr. C. I. Scofield and later by George L.
Alrich. Mrs. Elizabeth Needham wrote for years
a daily Scripture Calendar.

In 1893 a gentleman attended one of my Jewish meetings. He showed deep interest, though
he did not understand all that I said. This brother
was Mr. F. C. Jennings, a merchant and a devoted
Christian and able student of the Word of God.
He became a few years later our constant and most
valued contributor to the magazine. His able
expositions of Judges and Ruth, followed by
most helpful articles on Revelation and later
the book of Isaiah have helped thousands of
our readers. *Our Hope* is still leading among
the Bible Study magazines published, though they
have increased in considerable numbers.

The first book I published was *Studies in
Zechariah*. It has gone through nearly twenty
editions, and has been published in a German

translation in Germany. As this exposition contains so much about Christ, His first and His second coming, I sent a free copy to every Jewish Rabbi in New York and vicinity, but I never heard a word from any of them. One day I noticed a young Hebrew in my Temple Court Bible Reading. He paid splendid attention and became a regular attendant. I spoke to him, and he said that he was the Secretary of Rabbi . . . . "One day," this young man said, "the Rabbi received a book in the mail. He read it for a while and then fired it into the waste paper basket. I took it home with me. This book opened my eyes, and I believe Jesus is our Messiah and my Saviour." The book was *Studies in Zechariah.*

For thirty years now I have written book after book, thousands of which have been put into libraries and circulated free among preachers and missionaries.

I mention briefly the different works and their character.

The Gospel of Matthew, a complete exposition of the entire Gospel consisting of two volumes of over six hundred pages, has been published in many editions and is recognized as one of the best commentaries on the kingly Gospel. *The Harmony of the Prophetic Word* is a key to the Word of Prophecy in both Testaments. It has been used especially with young preachers. Scores of them have written that it was used to open their eyes to the truth of the Lord's coming. The late Dr. Clarence W. Weyer, pastor of the First Presbyterian Church of Tacoma, Wash., told me that the study of this volume had revolutionized his preaching. *The Prophet Daniel*, written and published in 1912, has gone through many editions of tens of thousands of copies. When published, it was welcomed by the leading Bible teachers as the most helpful exposition of the visions and prophecies of Daniel. Among those who wrote glowing tributes were Sir Robert Anderson of London, Walter Scott, C. I. Scofield, W. H. Griffith Thomas, and others. A large edition in the Spanish language was published, and many Bible classes were started in Spanish speaking countries through missionaries to whom we sent free copies of the book. An Italian edition was mostly circulated among the Waldensian Christians. *The Book of Revelation.* This volume has had an equally large circulation; over forty thousand were printed like my *Daniel* also in Spanish and in Italian. *The Prophet Joel*, one of the very few expositions of this book, has found a welcome among earnest students of the Scriptures.

The Prophet Ezekiel fills a real want in the interpretation of the prophetic portions of the Old Testament. Chapter by chapter is analyzed and explained. *The Gospel of John* is one of my latest expository works covering the entire Gospel, a volume of over four hundred pages. *The Book of Acts* has gone through seven editions and is very popular with Sunday-School teachers. *Unsearchable Riches* is a complete exposition of the Epistle to the Ephesians. The first three chapters had been previously published as *The Masterpiece of God.* *The Work of Christ* contains a setting forth of the past, the present, and future work of our Lord. *Types in Joshua* unfolds the typical teachings of the first part of Joshua. *Christianity or Religion?* is the result of five years' study in the origin and development of religion; it demonstrates the supernatural character of Christianity. This work was published as a challenge to modernism, but the argument developed in this volume has never been met by any scholar of the evolutionary theology. It is in the third edition and has been published in large editions in Chinese, Spanish, German, Bulgarian, and Swedish. *The Lord of Glory* contains devotional essays on the Person and Glory of the Lord Jesus Christ. *The Church in the House* was printed in response to many requests to publish a series of my sermons.

The Jewish Question unfolds the past, the present, and the future of Israel in the light of Romans xi. Many Jews have greatly enjoyed the reading of this volume. The late Ex-President Grover Cleveland, after reading this book, sent me a personal letter stating how profitable it was to him.

I mention six smaller volumes. I call them *The Pine Hill Books*. I shall speak of my summer sanctum, Pine Hill, later. But here in seclusion and undisturbed I wrote *The Angels of God*, a book of cheer and comfort; *The Healing Question*, answering the fanatical faith-healing cults; *The Holy Spirit*, which contains a brief setting forth of the Doctrine of the Holy Spirit; *The Return of the Lord*, in which every passage in the New Testament relating to our Lord's Return is quoted and explained. *Prayer* also goes through both Testaments showing the great place prayer holds in the lives of the Saints of God. *The Christ We Know* has in it some thirty devotional studies, and is a good answer to a certain audacious book with the title, *The Man Nobody Knows*. *Studies in Prophecy* is a series of lectures.

But my greatest work is the *Annotated Bible*. It was begun in 1912 and completed ten years later. It covers the entire Bible in nine volumes of over 3,000 pages. The production of this work demanded a vast amount of research and reading. The construction is as follows: An introduction to each Bible book. The arguments of destructive criticism are examined and answered. External and internal evidences are given, proving the authorship and authenticity of the different books;

the objections made by modernistic scholars are answered. This is followed by a careful division of the book itself. Here the purpose of each book is examined and the main divisions and subdivisions are pointed out.

Then follow Analyses and Annotations. Each chapter is divided as to its contents. The annotations cover more than historical facts and doctrines. Spiritual and dispensational truths are unfolded from Genesis to Revelation. Students of prophecy are finding this Bible work most helpful. The fanciful interpretations of which certain teachers of prophecy are often guilty are not found in the *Annotated Bible*. Its great value consists in simplicity and in the avoidance of elaborate detail. It is a work of comparative and progressive Bible Study.

Glowing words of appreciation and endorsement were received at the completion of the work from Professor Charles R. Erdman, D.D., of Princeton; Charles A. Blanchard, D.D., of Wheaton College; Professor Leander S. Keyser, D.D.; Dr. James M. Gray; Dr. Reuben A. Torrey, and many others. Dr. C. I. Scofield on receiving the first volume wrote.

> It is a pleasure to welcome and commend this first volume of Mr. Gaebelein's great work, the *Annotated Bible*. The present volume covers the Pentateuch. Over this part of the Holy Scriptures, as all are aware, the critical conflict of the last forty years has ranged. Every resource of human

learning, of skilled dialectics, of unbelief arrogating to itself the great name of Science, has been brought to bear upon the task of discrediting the divine authority and origin of these five books. Mr. Gaebelein is fortunate in the time in which he writes. The battle is over. From mere exhaustion of material and even of conjecture no new thing is being said. It is possible, therefore, to look over the scene of the conflict, and to estimate without heat of controversy the real weight of the critical arguments.

Mr. Gaebelein writes from the standpoint of an unhesitating faith in the integrity, inspiration, Mosaic authorship and authority of these ancient oracles. But he makes it evident that his faith is neither ignorant nor unreasoning. He has weighed the arguments and alleged facts of the higher criticism fairly, and presents an admirable summary of the critical conclusions.

As an apologetic of great present cogency and value I know of nothing at once so clear, fair and convincing.

But his volume of *The Annotated Bible* is far more than an apologetic as against the higher criticism. Constructively, it presents admirable analyses of the five books, and clear, sane and spiritual interpretations of the great types. To those who have been repelled by wild allegorizing and forced interpretations of the types of Scripture, this part of Mr. Gaebelein's work will especially commend itself.

Several years later he said in a letter to me: "I marvel that you have accomplished so much of the *Annotated Bible* and rejoice that it is nearing its completion. When it can be given forth as a whole, it will, I feel sure, be in great demand. I will be glad to review it for the *Times* literary supplement and the *Herald*.

And here it is in place to mention the "Scofield

Reference Bible." The birthplace of this great work of our brother, now with the Lord, was Sea Cliff, Long Island. I shall speak of the Sea Cliff Conference, inaugurated and conducted by me, in the next chapter. Scofield, during the second Conference in 1902, spoke of producing such a work and during a long night-walk along the shore outlined the plan. The next day the matter was mentioned to our brethren, Francis E. Fitch, Alwyn Ball, Jr., John T. Pirie, and John B. Buss. All showed great enthusiasm. But it was the generosity of Alwyn Ball, Jr., which really made the work possible; the other brethren also helped liberally. Mr. Scofield went to Montreux, Switzerland, to begin his task. I had promised him every possible assistance by taking over certain sections of the Bible, furnishing the analysis of certain books and assisting in prophetic interpretations. A voluminous correspondence followed covering several years. A few years later when the work had been started he wrote:

"My beloved Brother: By all means follow your own views of prophetic analysis. I sit at your feet when it comes to prophecy and congratulate in advance the future readers of the Reference Bible on having in their hands a safe, clear, sane guide through what to most is a labyrinth.

"Yours lovingly in Christ,

"C. I. S."

THE NEW COMMISSION

A year before his home-call he asked me to make a revision of the Bible, correct anything which ought to be corrected, make additions, etc. I did so, but up to this time no revised edition has been printed.

I should also like to mention the 1911 Bible. The Oxford University Press sent me on November 6, 1909, an invitation to serve on a committee of scholars to go over the King James version to change obsolete phrases and make other changes which were absolutely necessary, disturbing as little as possible the authorized text. Among the others called were: Dr. E. Y. Mullins, Prof. Joseph Kyle, Robert Dick Wilson, Bishop Candler, John R. Raven and Dr. Weidner. They assigned to me the Minor Prophets. The 1911 commemorative edition was published by the Oxford University Press, but for some reason it never became popular.

I could not possibly mention all the smaller booklets which I wrote and which were circulated in many editions, but one I cannot pass by.

It was during a severe attack of illness, when weak in body, that I preached in Florida on 2 Cor. viii:9. I had to hold myself on the pulpit for fear of falling over. But, as so many times in my work, once more I found out the blessed truth, "My strength is made perfect in weakness." The Lord stood by me and gave such a great blessing to my own soul that I was melted in tears and the

audience was swept by a wave of blessing. I
felt the message must be enlarged and written
out. Thus *His Riches—Our Riches* came into
existence. This booklet of 72 pages has appeared
in about a million copies in English, German,
Spanish, French, Polish, Portugese, Bulgarian,
Russian, Bohemian, Italian, Dutch, Chinese, Kor-
ean, a Filipino Dialect, Mahrati, Bengali, Swedish,
Danish-Norwegian, and in Icelandic. It found
ready readers in these nineteen languages. Dr.
Arthur T. Pierson, to whom I had given the
manuscript to read, wrote: "This book is emi-
nently adapted to save sinners and to feed saints."
His prophecy has come true. During the war
copies were used by the tens of thousands in the
different camps. On the request of an English
officer in the army of General Allenby, when on
his way to Jerusalem, hundreds were sent and
distributed. Scores of letters reached me from
the trenches and the boys wrote of the great
blessing they had received. I have not kept
track of the persons who wrote me that the
booklet resulted in their salvation. About 100,000
have gone forth in Spanish and have been circulated in every Spanish-speaking country. And
still the requests come for it. One of the striking
cases is that of a young Indian girl who read it
in Peru. She was taken ill with typhus and
taken to a Roman Catholic Hospital. The priests
and nuns tried their best to shake her simple

faith. She quoted in Spanish from "His Riches," and before she passed away recited in Spanish, "Just as I am, without one plea, but that Thy blood was shed for me." This Gospel message has warmed the hearts of the Icelanders, and brought light and salvation to Hindus, and stirred Slavonic races, and it is still doing its work. Whole families have been led to Christ. A dear saint said, after reading this message, "God would not be God, if He did not bless this booklet."

Traveling in the far West, I noticed a Catholic priest in the Pullman. I engaged him in conversation and handed him a copy of *His Riches*, which he promised to read. When he had finished it, he came with tears in his eyes and said: "I felt this morning a desire for something which would be of spiritual help to me, and God has answered my desire through this little book. It was water for my thirsty soul, for it presents the purest Gospel in such a beautiful way. I want to thank you for it." He wrote on it, "Every good Catholic ought to read it and benefit by it."

Many times have I been asked how I managed to write so many books, produce the *Annotated Bible*, and travel from coast to coast. The answer is very simple. I never wasted time. "Do you play golf?" "No." "Why not?" "Not because it is wrong, but because I can use my time in a better way." Doing the work systematically is another secret of my success. It is also true that for some sixteen years I never took a vacation, but kept at it summer and winter. But the real reason is His mercy and His kindness in giving me the needed strength both spiritually and physically. And so to Him be all the glory!

PART IV

FROM COAST TO COAST

CHAPTER VIII

ALTHOUGH I had done much traveling, holding Bible Conferences here and there during the years of 1896-1900, the larger ministry began with the first year of the Twentieth Century. To cover all these years and mention every place where it has been my privilege to minister is quite impossible. I shall take the reader with me to the most prominent places. We shall travel together from coast to coast. Before we do this I should like to make some general remarks on the ministry which it has been my happy privilege to render in the body of Christ.

Ministry is of the Lord. "When He ascended upon high, He led captivity captive, and gave gifts unto men . . . and He gave some apostles; and some prophets, and some evangelists; and some pastors and teachers" (Ephes. iv:10, 12). It pleased Him to grant unto me the gift of a teacher. But at the same time the work of an evangelist and pastor, shepherding the flock of God, has also been done by me. All through these years in holding Bible Conferences, monthly meetings and other services, the preaching of the Gospel was never neglected. I recall no Lord's Day evening during my ministry when I did not preach Christ. Needless to say I could not follow the methods of the professional evangelist. There never was any "trail-hitting" in my Gospel ministry; nor did I indulge in the other, often questionable methods, of forcing people to accept God's offer of salvation. My trust has always been in the work of the Holy Spirit in connection with the preaching of the Gospel of His Grace. Many times there seemed to be no result. Nobody came to confess Christ. But many, many times weeks and months, and even years after, I received letters from those who had accepted the Gospel and were saved. How wonderfully this confirmed me in my faith in the quickening power of the Holy Spirit!

In His letter to the Church in Philadelphia, the faithful remnant during the last days of the present age, the Head of the Church, our Lord, gives the promise, "I have set before thee an open door, and no man can shut it" (Rev. iii:8). This was my great comfort—that He opens doors. Next to my childhood verse of calling upon Him in the day of trouble, I have seen the most startling fulfilment of this Philadelphian promise. Laodicea is all about us. It is the final state of Protestant Christendom, lukewarm, indifferent, and modernistic. Yet the work of the true servant of God is not to denounce the professing Church, but to go and bear a loving, faithful testimony to those in Laodicea. In apostolic days there was a servant of Christ who did this work. It was and is my earnest desire to follow his example. His name was Epaphras. What a testimony the Holy Spirit gave as to his work! "For I bear him record, that he has a great zeal for you, and them that are in Laodicea, and them in Hierapolis" (Col. iv:13). Door after door was opened. Dr. Scofield, who followed my ministry more closely than anybody else, wrote me words of encouragement.

He said in the beginning of the Twentieth Century: "What a wonderful ministry our God is giving you! Blessed be His precious name for His gift of you to His body. See how quickly He honors one who takes a place with Him outside of Laodicea, but still loving and seeking to serve 'any man' in Laodicea who has a heart for Him. It is most blessed, but also most humbling to think that in *us*—in even such as we—He goes in to sup with His own, that He lets *us* pass the bread and the fishes still. Who is sufficient for these things?"

And this was the constant cry of my heart, "Who is sufficient for these things? Keep me humble! Lord, keep me humble! Let me be nothing; be Thou all! Not unto me but unto Thee be the glory! Keep me from seeking the glory which comes from man!" These were my prayers for all these years, and they are still the prayers of my heart.

Let us then begin and trace this God-given, Spirit-led ministry from coast to coast.

New England. This has been one of the best fields of my ministry. As *Boston* is called "The Hub," we shall begin with this good, old city. My first visit was made in 1884. In the early nineties I met, in connection with the Christian and Missionary Alliance work, Mr. Clark W. Morehouse. We became close friends, and his good home in Union Park Street was always open to me. Different visits were made by me to address meetings planned by Brother Morehouse. I also became acquainted with Dr. A. J. Gordon of the Clarendon Street Baptist Church and preached for him. In 1894 I delivered an address in the Park Street Congregational Church, the first time I spoke in this historic building, and as already stated, Dr. Niles invited me frequently to address meetings of Jews in a rented hall in Kneeland Street. This was followed by the Prophetic Conference held in Berkeley Temple. But the real Boston testimony began in 1901. Dr. Scofield was then the pastor of the Church in East Northfield. I wrote him about holding a three days' conference in the Park Street Congregational Church in February of 1901. He gave his promise to come during the first week in February of 1901. I rented the lecture room and we had a most blessed Conference over the Word of God. Besides Dr. Scofield, John M. Carnie, an evangelist, and I, were the speakers. Mr. and Mrs. Francis E. Fitch, Mr. and Mrs. Alwyn Ball had come from New York to attend this

Conference, and there was great blessing. Before the meetings were over numerous people requested more meetings of the same nature. One said, "Could you not come once a month from New York and give us an all day meeting?" This suggestion proved valuable. I made there and then the arrangement for a meeting on every first Thursday of the month, and for twenty-eight years these monthly meetings have been held in the Park Street Church. They are still going on, though in a different place. This started a kind of a "Monthly Meeting Movement" all over the country.

Besides these monthly gatherings, I had an annual Bible Conference for Boston and New England, which was largely attended. I only missed the year 1930 in holding such a conference. Among the speakers of these conferences were: James M. Gray, A. C. Dixon, C. I. Scofield, Arthur T. Pierson, George L. Alrich, John M. Carnie, F. C. Jennings, Donald D. Monro, Hugh R. Monro, Don O. Shelton, Arthur F. Wells, Sidney T. Smith, A. Gordon MacLennan, Herbert Bieber, Frank E. Gaebelein, and others. These meetings have brought untold blessings to saints and sinners. When recently I was in doubt whether I should continue, scores of our Boston friends urged their continuation.

I ministered in different cities of *Maine*. In *New Hampshire* I held meetings in *Gorham, Rochester, Lakeport, Laconia, Manchester* and

Nashua. In *Massachusetts* I held for ten years German meetings in *Lawrence,* the place where my servantship started. Besides addressing large meetings in German I addressed smaller gatherings. *Haverhill* was visited almost monthly for a whole year. In *Lowell, Lynn, Salem, Peabody* and several smaller towns my testimony was given to gatherings of believers. *Worcester* also was visited for a number of years regularly. A beloved brother, a devoted Christian, Mr. Jonathan Prescott Grosvenor, had started a Mission in memory of Pauline, a daughter. Here my first testimony was given. Later conferences were held in different churches, and still later we had services in Mr. Grosvenor's good home. God's blessing was much in evidence in Worcester. For a time *Springfield* was also regularly visited and in the middle of the last decade of the nineteenth century I made regular visits to Brockton and ministered the Word in Olivet Chapel. Only once did I visit *East Northfield,* preaching for my friend, Dr. Scofield, in the East Northfield Congregational Church; this was when Mr. Moody was still here. He recognized the blessing which my ministry had brought.

All the other New England States, except *Vermont,* were covered by my ministry. In *Rhode Island* I held conferences in *Providence* and *Pawtucket.* In *Connecticut,* I spoke in *Bridgeport, New Haven, New Britain, Stamford* and *Greenwich.*

In *Hartford* I held a week's meetings in the Y. M. C. A., and something of interest happened during that week. There lived in Hartford a cultured old lady, Mrs. Beecher Hooker, I believe a half sister of Henry Ward Beecher. Her home, I was told, was a kind of shrine of cultured New Englanders. One day a lady appeared at the Y. M. C. A., and said: "I have a great surprise for you. Mrs. Beecher Hooker has heard of you. She wants to meet you, and asks you to dine with her on Thursday noon. And I want to tell you this is considered a great honor here in Hartford, for Mrs. Hooker only invites a certain class of men to her table, like Dr. Lyman Abbott, Theodore Roosevelt, and President Taft as her guests."

And so I went and found a venerable, white-haired old lady, who received me very kindly. She wanted to know something about the Jews and seemed to be interested in their future.

There were several other guests, and during the dinner she turned to me and made the following statements: "Do you not think that it is encouraging to find that our fair New England is turning more and more away from that awful teaching that a human being can get to heaven through the blood of another man?" She waited a moment, and, as I did not answer, she continued, "As if the blood of an innocent victim could do any good to anybody. It is our character, our life which tells. This is the true Gospel."

I had to speak. I knew it would be rude to challenge her statements and to contradict her, for I was a guest at her table. But I said to myself, "I would rather be rude than to have my Lord insulted." As soon as I made this inward conclusion, there came power and courage to witness.

I said, "Mrs. Beecher Hooker, I have listened to your words, and while you spoke I thought, 'If the great preacher Lyman Beecher had listened, what would he say to your words?'" The old lady turned pale. "And Mrs. Beecher Hooker, what about the Hookers of your state of two hundred years ago, who preached the cross and the blood as the only means of acceptance with God?" She got red and did not open her lips. "Oh, let me tell you, Mrs. Hooker, unless you are washed in the blood of the Lamb you will never see heaven. You are very old, soon you must pass on, and I can assure you your character cannot save you." She had not much to say after that, and was silent. When I left, a lady who was present followed me, and, with tears in her eyes, she said, "Oh! how I thank God that you gave her the truth. She has made this speech at her table for several years and all her guests were silent; you are the only man who has contradicted her and given her the Gospel." A short time after she passed away. Perhaps my testimony was not in vain.

What blessing everywhere! In numerous places my work was that of a pioneer. While evangelistic

meetings had been held before, Bible Conferences, constructive Bible teaching, were quite
unknown. It was a great joy to me when people,
after hearing me on His glorious return, came
up and said that they never had heard a sermon
before on the second coming of Christ, and then
I had the satisfaction to see how they were led
out into the light of "that blessed hope".

Our home state, the Empire State, *New York*,
has been and still is the scene of my activity. Let
me begin with the greatest and finest city of the
United States.

The Temple Court meetings have been recorded
before. I should like to add that, while these meetings were small, their influence was very wide, for
frequently business men dropped in from different
parts of the country and received much light
and help through the ministry. Many similar
meetings in halls and private homes were held
by me throughout all these years. Among these
I mention the home of the late Mrs. Cyrus de
Peyster Field on Madison Square, where a company of earnest believers gathered week after
week for many years. I preached in numerous
Methodist, Baptist, Reformed and other Christian churches in different parts of Manhattan
and Brooklyn. In Brooklyn, in 1902 and 1903,
I held two Bible Conferences in the Y. W. C. A.
on Flatbush Avenue and Schermerhorn Street.
They were well attended. The speakers included,

besides myself, Arthur T. Pierson, Dr. C. I. Scofield, F. C. Jennings and John M. Carnie. In 1903, I held the first New York Bible Conference in the Y. M. C. A. Building on Fourth Avenue and Twenty-third Street. The attendance was fine, and Dr. Scofield spoke twice daily with myself and Mr. F. C. Jennings. Passing over many meetings and conferences held from time to time in the city, I speak especially of the great Carnegie Hall Bible and Prophetic Conference in 1918. It was one of the high points of my Christian activity.

In 1913 on my suggestion, a Prophetic Conference was planned for February, 1914, to be held in the Moody Church of *Chicago*. Dr. James M. Gray took up this suggestion and the conference was held, and became the source of the widest influence for good. But nobody knew that before 1914 ended the beginning of a great world-war would have passed into history. The Chicago Conference was certainly ordered by the Lord. In the early part of 1918 I spoke to Mr. Alwyn Ball, Jr., and to several other brethren, about holding in the Fall during the Thanksgiving week another Prophetic Bible Conference. The suggestion was enthusiastically received, and a committee was formed at once. But nobody knew that in November the war would end. Carnegie Hall, the biggest hall of New York seating over 4,000, was secured and I wrote and issued a call signed by almost

100 New York preachers, business and professional men. We began advertising at once. It will be of interest to reprint part of this call, for it has some historical significance.

Over four years ago the horrible world-conflict started, a conflict which has filled the earth with unspeakable suffering. Since then millions have asked the questions, 'How is it all going to end— Is this to go on forever or is there something better in store for the human race and for this earth?' Who can give us a definite answer? There is but one book in existence which answers these all important questions. That book is the Bible, of which recently our President bore witness, that it is the Word of God, the Word of life. In the inspired pages of the Bible we find the prophetic record of a coming day when all swords will be turned into plowshares and all spears into pruning-hooks. It is in this blessed Book we read of nations learning war no more, and that ultimately the human race, freed from the curse which sin has brought, will enjoy permanent peace. Yea, the very glory of the Lord is to cover the earth as the waters cover the deep. How and when all this will come to pass is also made known in this Divine revelation. The present day upheavals seem to many to be the travail pains of the birth of that coming age of righteousness and peace.

It behooves us, therefore, to turn to this sacred Book and to examine its great teachings as never before. We, therefore, cordially and earnestly invite all Christians, irrespective of creed or denomi-nation, as well as non-Christians to meet with us in a conference over the Word of God and to listen to the testimony of a number of well-known minis-ters of the Lord Jesus Christ, of various denomina-tions, who will unfold with the gracious help of the Spirit of God the great prophetic truths of the Bible. This Conference will meet, God willing, from Monday, November 25th, to Thursday,

November 28th, inclusive, in Carnegie Hall, 57th Street and Seventh Avenue, New York City.

The signers of this invitation are a guarantee that this Conference will offer no opportunity for a certain class of teachers to advance their fanciful speculations and unscriptural theories, or to give expression to any sentiment not in fullest loyalty to our country and her allies. But this occasion will be used to give prominence to the prophetic forecasts of the Word of God, to warn against present day apostasy, to sound forth the midnight cry once more 'Behold, He Cometh,' and with it present the most majestic of all motives for world wide evangelism, to call attention to the great doctrines of the Gospel as a bulwark and a protest against the subtle skepticism of the German-made theology, and to bring into closer fellowship all those 'who love His Appearing.' It is also planned to give a special testimony on the future of the Jewish people, whose star of hope now shines so brightly.

I received not a little ridicule from certain men who thought it foolish that a place like Carnegie Hall should be rented for four hundred dollars per day to hold a prophetic conference. One prominent preacher said: "You Premillennialists think that everybody will run after you. If you fill the lower floor of the hall, you will do well."

I was late in coming to the first meeting to deliver the opening address on "The Pre-eminence of the Lord Jesus Christ." Charles Alexander was leading in a spirited way the singing. A few minutes later one of the Carnegie Hall officers came and informed me that the seating capacity of the hall was exhausted and he said, "There are several hundred outside whom we cannot let in on account of the instructions from the fire department." I looked into the sea of faces and one of the first I saw was the preacher who had ridiculed holding such a conference. He leaned against a pillar unable to find a seat.

As I arose to speak, there was a great hush. But before long I was interrupted by loud "Amens" and repeatedly I had to stop on account of the applause. Dr. Torrey followed me. J. Wilbur Chapman, the great Evangelist, after the conference was over gave to the press the following account:

"New York is in the midst of great rejoicing because of the prospect of peace. It goes without saying that the city is more stirred up than I have ever known it to be, and I have been a resident for twenty years.

"It would naturally seem that such a time as this was hardly favorable for a Prophetic Bible Conference, or indeed for a Bible Conference of any kind, and there were some thoughtful Christians in the city who looked with some questioning upon the proposal, but the meetings have been held and it would be impossible to describe the profound impression which has been made by the Conference. Dr. A. C. Gaebelein, more than anyone else, was responsible for this Conference. It was much on his mind and heart to hold such a conference, and he felt led of God to lay his plans before a committee of business men. This committee consisted of such men as Delavan Pierson, Alwyn Ball, Jr., Hugh R. Monro, George H. Dowkontt, J. A. Richards, Charles E. Gremmels, George W. Carter, H. W. Strong, Charles Young and Oscar C. Rixson. Carnegie Hall was crowded to the doors and every night it was necessary to hold several overflow meetings in nearby churches.

"Among the speakers were A. C. Gaebelein, R. A. Torrey, James M. Gray, W. B. Riley, W. H. Griffiths Thomas, Joseph W. Kemp, J. Wilbur Chapman, Ford C. Ottman, Otho Bartholow, David Burrell, Leon Tucker, W. L. Pettingill and others.

"There is a readiness on the part of Christian people to listen to this testimony, such as I have not seen in many years, and the great hall filled to overflowing with eager, expectant, praying, singing people, reminded me of nothing so much as the old days when D. L. Moody was at the height of his power preaching the Gospel as no one ever did."

Besides the Carnegie Hall meetings we held every morning a meeting in the Collegiate Reformed Church, Fifth Avenue and Twenty-ninth Street. Here, too, the meetings were filled to overflowing. The influences of this great Conference, though it is twelve years after, are still felt.

President Wilson had been invited by me to express his sympathy with the Conference. I received a courteous reply stating that, on account of his early departure for France, he had not the time to send a larger personal message, but he sent a pamphlet containing an address on the Bible, part of which was quoted by me in the opening address. Vice-President Marshall sent a personal letter to me, which was also read.

Among those who presided over the meetings were my life-long friend, Williams Philips Hall, President of the American Tract Society, John E. Milholland, and Dr. Otho Bartholow, of Mount Vernon, N. Y.

During the war I addressed thousands of the boys. One meeting held in *Fort Slocum* on Long Island Sound was remarkable. A large number of soldiers were training there, ready to leave for France. The Y. M. C. A. Secretary seemed to me nervous and cautioned me not to be too long in my address. He said, "They are restless and they may all go out." So they had a song, and then the Secretary announced that they would have a wonderful moving picture show, which they all would enjoy. "But before we show the pictures, this gentleman will say a few words to you." And, as I got up to speak, he whispered, "Not more than ten minutes." I announced my text, "Almost thou persuadest me to be a Christian" (Acts xxvi:28). After speaking a few sentences, I felt that I had the whole soldier audience with me. Their eyes fairly hung on my lips. After picturing the scene of Paul before Agrippa and giving them the historical background, I spoke on how we become Christians and what it means to be a Christian. Such attention I have rarely seen. Well, I spoke four times ten minutes, in fact about forty-five minutes. When I reached the end of the discourse, I said, "How many boys want to become real Christians tonight by accepting the Lord Jesus Christ? Will you come forward and kneel down in front? And when we are gathered here, I shall pray with you and for you." My lips had hardly closed when about a hundred or more came to the front, and all knelt down while I prayed. I believe from the way they later took me by the hand, and the way they expressed themselves, that many were saved. Then the Secretary got up and expressed his great pleasure over the meeting, announcing that the next number on he program was the movies. But he had a surprise. Three-fourths of the boys arose and left the hall.

In camps and on ships *His Riches* was circulated in great quantities. In *Our Hope*, October, 1917, I find the following note: "We have offered 25,000 copies to the War Commission of the Presbyterian Church through Dr. J. Wilbur Chapman. They will be used among drafted men. We offered them in lots of thousands to Dr. Mark A. Matthews for distribution at Bremerton, Fort Worden, Fort Lawton, and the Naval Training Station."

And now a word about the *Sea Cliff Bible Con-*

ferences. These were planned in 1901, the year
in which the first conference was held. There were
several reasons why Sea Cliff, some 28 miles
from New York on Long Island Sound, was selected. Mr. John T. Pirie had his summer estate
here, and when I asked him about holding such
meetings every summer, he agreed enthusiastically
and offered a large plot in the center of the village.
A big tent was secured and the first Conference
convened July 23-29. It was a time of great
blessing. Dr. Scofield was especially used in giving four great addresses on "Where Faith Sees
Christ." Other speakers, besides myself, were
George L. Alrich, F. C. Jennings, John M. Carnie.
Through the generosity of Mr. Fitch, a 15,000
copy edition of *Our Hope* was printed, containing the full report of this first conference. For
ten years these conferences were continued. Other
speakers were Walter Scott, W. W. Fereday, both
of Great Britain; Ford C. Ottman, L. W. Munhall,
and others. Each conference was fully reported
in the September issues of *Our Hope.* The
attendants came from different states and from
Canada. When Mr. John T. Pirie went home to
be with the Lord, we discontinued the Sea Cliff
Conferences. The present day Sea Cliff meetings
are not the successor of the original conference.

Traveling eastward on Long Island some twenty-
five miles from Sea Cliff we come to *Stony Brook,*
an old village dating back to revolutionary times.

Here under the leadership of the late Dr. John F. Carson, pastor of the Central Presbyterian Church and one of the former moderators of the General Assembly, a large tract of land had been purchased with the thought of establishing summer Bible Conferences. Associated with him were the late Dr. Ford C. Ottman and Dr. David G. Wylie. An auditorium seating about a thousand people had been built. Mr. Robert Johnston donated a hall, known as Johnston Hall. Another friend of the movement, Mr. Ferdinand T. Hopkins, had erected Hopkins Hall. It has been my privilege to be identified with the conference work in Stony Brook for twenty years.

In 1920 much was said about establishing a boys' preparatory school in which the Bible should have its rightful place in the curriculum and which would stand for positive Christianity. Such a school seemed one of the greatest needs of our times, so that boys of Christian homes might be saved from the clutches of the infidels in cap and gown, whose aim seems to be to destroy the faith of the young in a supernatural Bible.

In 1921 my youngest son Frank, after having received his Master's degree in English from Harvard University, decided to devote his life to Christian education. When Dr. Carson met him for the first time, he said enthusiastically, "Our problem is solved; we have the man who will help us in this movement." Frank, though only in his twenty-second year, rented a small office in the Presbyterian Building, 156 Fifth Avenue, and began the necessary steps in the foundation of the school. As the motto for the school, *Character Before Career* was adopted. It was, however, fully recognized that a true Christian character cannot be formed apart from the Gospel of Jesus Christ.

The inauguration of the school took place on Wednesday, September 13, 1922. Dr. Carson presided. Among the speakers were Dr. M. A. Abbott of Lawrenceville School; L. P. Powell, ex-President of Hobart College. Then the youngest headmaster in the country, Frank E. Gaebelein, delivered an address on "The Purpose and Scope of the Stony Brook School." He was followed by one of the oldest and most able educators of our time, Dr. Francis L. Patton, former President of Princeton University.

As I am not writing the history of Stony Brook, I do not follow this movement. But I must say that the Stony Brook School in its success and development is almost a miracle. God's blessing has rested upon it in a wonderful way.

The city of *Buffalo* I must mention next, for I did more work there than in any other city of our state, except New York itself. My first meetings were held in 1897. A good looking Scotchman presided. He was an earnest Christian and a forceful speaker. Thus I met for the first

time my friend Edward Fairbairn, whose fellowship I have enjoyed now for almost thirty-
five years. Another Conference was held in
1901, and Mr. Alwyn Ball, Jr. came along to take
part. On my suggestion Mr. Fairbairn inaugurated monthly meetings which were held for a
number of years in the Y. W. C. A. building. I
made many visits and also preached in the Prospect Ave. Baptist Church, the First Baptist
Church, and other churches. An influential member of the Richmond Avenue Methodist Church
succeeded in getting permission to hold a week's
meetings in this church, which was considered
very fashionable. The pastor was much displeased and after having listened for a week to
straightforward Bible teaching, including the premillennial coming of the Lord, he was reported
as having said, "After all this Calvinistic perse-
verance of the Saints and premillennial talk I
think my pulpit ought to be fumigated." Needless to say no other invitation ever came to me
from this church. The monthly meetings developed into the City Mission movement, of which
Mr. E. Clark was the superintendent. I made
yearly visits to Buffalo to hold Bible Conferences
in the Mission and in Assembly Hall on Elmwood
Avenue, which had been erected under the leadership of Mr. Fairbairn. I still continue in my
visits to Buffalo.

FROM COAST TO COAST

Elmira, N. Y. In 1896 the N. Y. State Convention of the Christian Endeavor Society was held in Park Church. I received an invitation to address the 3,000 young people who had gathered. Among the other speakers was Dr. A. C. Dixon.

After my address a young man, Mr. Casper G. Decker, came up to greet me and take me to his home. We became friends, and have been intimate friends ever since.

Numerous conferences have been held by me in the Hedding M. E. Church and in the Y. M. C. A. During this year (1930) I conducted a Conference in the Riverside M. E. Church which brought blessing to many.

I can only mention other places of our great State without going into details. *Auburn, N. Y.,* was visited several times, also *Ithaca, Watertown, Johnstown* and *Gloversville.* Many visits were made to *Rochester, N. Y. Binghamton, Nyack, Yonkers, Tarrytown, Oxford,* and other towns were visited by me to scatter the precious seed.

In our capital city, *Albany,* I held conferences for a number of years and preached in different churches. Most of my conferences there were held in a German Reformed Church.

For about eight years I have ministered in a number of the smaller villages of Ulster and Delaware Counties. I mention them: *Kings-*

ton, Phoenicia, Chichester, Shandaken, Pine Hill, Fleishmanns (called on account of its Jewish summer population "the Jerusalem of the Cats-kills"), *Margaretville, Andes, Walton, Roxbury* and *Prattsville.*

But what led me to minister in villages of a few hundred inhabitants and that as a labor of love? It is an interesting story showing the kindness of Him whom I serve, who is still the same as He ever was, who still speaks to His toiling servants, "Come ye yourselves apart and rest awhile."

In 1921 on my way to the South I noticed an advertisement in a magazine that the country estate of the late Dr. Wm. H. McCracken, Chancellor of New York University, was for sale. I knew its location and the charming mountain country where it is situated.

Arriving in Baton Rouge, La., I was enter-tained in the home of Mr. and Mrs. Amos K. Gordon and called attention to this advertisement, suggesting that it would be a splendid thing to take the family there during the hot summer months. It resulted in Mr. Gordon, who is the Vice-President of the Standard Oil Co. of Louisi-ana, purchasing the estate. As there are two houses on the property, the Gordons very kindly put one of these houses at our disposal, and so for nine years the Lord graciously provided what I needed, quietness and rest during the heated term. What a blessing it has been to me cannot be expressed in words. It has kept me in health. It has enabled me to read and study undisturbed; it fitted me for the next season's strenuous work, Next to God's Word I love to study His other great Book, where He has revealed Himself and where He speaks to our heart—Nature. I love all His Works. I love the beautiful! And here was the great field of study in forests, in meadows. along the babbling mountain brooks, on mountain tops, and in deep glens. What lessons I have learned! And here the Lord enriched me in the knowledge of His truth, and eight of my books were written in the quietness of the Birch Creek Valley. And to be really apostolic I also had to go afishing!

Nor must I forget the delightful fellowship we enjoy in this mountain valley. Every night the Gordons and Mrs. Gaebelein and myself, visitors and servants, meet for the reading of the Word of God and a brief exposition, followed by prayer. And every Lord's Day afternoon there is a special service. But what my ministry has meant to these country villages in helping people in the knowledge of His Truth, I do not know. The coming day will declare it.

But I have not mentioned many other places throughout the Empire State where I have sown the seed of His Word.

CHAPTER IX

*P*ASSAIC and *Rutherford, N. J.*, have already been mentioned. These two places can never leave my memory, for there beloved friends stood nobly by me when my new commission was being carried out.

Many visits have been made to *Paterson* with its big Holland population. I have held conferences in different Holland Churches as well as in the "Star of Hope Mission," carried on so successfully by Mr. Peter Stam. A conference was held many years ago in the Madison Avenue Baptist Church when Mr. George Douglass was pastor. Since then I have enjoyed fellowship with Brother Edward Drew, the present pastor of this live church and have preached frequently for them. *Perth Amboy, New Brunswick, Princeton, Elizabeth, Newark, Atlantic City, Jersey City* and *Tenafly*, besides smaller places in the State of New Jersey have received my ministry, and here and there Bible classes have been established through my testimony.

I ministered in the Keystone State, *Pennsylvania*, in about thirty localities. Early in the Jewish work in 1894 I visited *Philadelphia* and frequently addressed good audiences of Jews. We had located a branch of our testimony to the

Jews in the Quaker City and Mr. Mark Lev, a Hebrew believer, had charge of it. For a time I held monthly meetings, which were conducted like the Boston meetings. These monthly meetings were held in different churches. Several Bible Conferences were held by me in churches and halls, and in 1919 the late John E. Milholland of New York arranged a conference for me in one of the Baptist Churches and in the Wylie-Chambers Memorial Presbyterian Church. More recently I visited Philadelphia, holding conferences and monthly meetings for two years in the Bethany Presbyterian Church, the so-called "Wanamaker Church," because this great merchant prince was its leading spirit. These meetings were held at the request of the pastor, Dr. Gordon A. MacLennan, and the session.

Pittsburgh had a large place in my early ministry. I located a branch of the "Hope of Israel" in this city and it was carried on for a time. At the same time much ministry was done in different churches. I must mention one interesting case. On the bulletin board of one of the United Presbyterian Churches it was announced that I would give an address on the future fulfilment of the last Book of the Bible. It was a teaching meeting. Among the hearers was a stranger, who had passed the church and who wrote later that he had been a professional gambler. He understood but little, but he was reminded that his godly mother used to read Revelation more than anything else and often talked about it. He left the service with the desire to read this book through and on the next day he purchased a Bible. He read the book and it resulted in his conversion. This shows the power of the Word of God. Some think that sinners can only be reached when a definite Gospel message is preached, but the Holy Spirit can reach the lost through any portion of the written Word of which He is the author.

In Central Pennsylvania I addressed in 1899 an enormous Camp Meeting of the Pennsylvania Dutch farmers. There must have been over three thousand present. The Pennsylvania Dutch are an interesting people. Their forbears came over from Germany several hundred years ago in the seventeenth century. They have kept up the German language, but it is the German of two hundred years ago. Furthermore, in speaking this German dialect they use English liberally, murdering the King's English as they do the German. It is for the philologist an interesting jargon, somewhat akin to the Yiddish-German. Many a good laugh have I had over their speech. We say in English, "See how beautifully the sun sets." Said an old farmer to me, "*Kuk amohl wie schoen die Sonn sich niedersetzt*," which literally translated means, "Just look and see how fine the sun sits itself down." An old farmer drove

me back in his buggy to the railroad station. On
the way there he pointed to a farm house and
informed me that there lived a farmer who did
not speak Pennsylvania Dutch. At the small
station I had another surprise. A negro spoke
Pennsylvania Dutch fluently. Along with the
language they maintain the peculiar habits of
the seventeenth century Germany. One of these
is the belief in witchery, which they call
"verhexen." The court records of Central Pennsylvania are full of cases of accusations of witchery.
It has been my privilege to minister the Word
among these good people, many of whom are
excellent believers and lovers of the Word of God.

   *Scranton, Pittston, Carbondale, Scottdale, Wilkes-
Barre, Williamsport, Tyrone* and *Altoona* have
been some of the fields where I have sown the living
seed of the living and abiding Word of God. In
some of these cities numerous and regular visits
were made and blessed results followed. For
a time monthly meetings were held in *Johnstown,*
which I supplied frequently.

   Some twenty years ago under the leadership
of W. G. Hean of *Harrisburg,* a Bible Conference
Circuit was inaugurated. This circuit includes
Harrisburg, Lebanon, Reading and *Allentown.* A
few days' meetings are held in each place every
month. I have supplied this circuit no less than
nine times. Besides this I held several conferences in Allentown in one of the oldest and

largest Lutheran Churches in the State, the St. Paul's Lutheran Church. I must pass by *Lancaster, Butler, Grove City, Germantown, Pottstown, Norristown, Quakertown, York* and other towns and villages.

In 1901 I visited *Waynesboro*. Mr. Alwyn Ball accompanied me. I had great faith and rented the Opera House, because no church was open to me. An audience of about twenty greeted me in the big barn they called the opera house. Nearly all of them belonged to the sect of the Dunkards, wearing their peculiar dress, hats and bonnets. Yet the Lord did a great work there and the blessings which resulted are still felt. These good folks had no clear conception of the true way of salvation. One good lady thought she was lost. She had for a special occasion exchanged her little bonnet for a simple but more fashionable hat. The Dunkard brethren had found it out. To them it was an evidence that she had become worldly, and so she was put out of fellowship. I told her, "Your salvation does not depend on what kind of a hat you wear. It depends on the finished work of Christ and your faith in Him." A few years later the Lord gave a larger ministry in this town, as the large Trinity Lutheran Church opened its doors and I held two successful conferences.

In 1922, my friend Dr. Reuben A. Torrey, requested me to take a week each year in connection with the *Montrose Bible Conference Association* and conduct a conference for the study of prophecy. This I have done for eight years and hope to do till my Lord and Master calls me to meet Him. These conferences have steadily increased and all the daily teaching is done by me.

Wilmington, Delaware, I visited but once, but *Baltimore,* my dear old Baltimore, has come in for a large share of my activities. The reader remembers that I had my first pastorate here in 1883-84. In 1897 I visited Baltimore on the invitation of Dr. Howard A. Kelly, with whom a friendship was then formed and on another visit I met, I think the same year, in a Y. M. C. A. Conference one of the best friends I have ever had, Mr. Gustavus Ober. Mr. Ober was one of heaven's noblemen. He was a fine Christian gentleman. From 1900-1912 we were together a great deal and many of my week-ends during the summers were spent in Baltimore. Mr. Ober was vitally interested in the *Port Mission* in the Southern part of the city. It was and is a mission to reach the seamen, as well as the large population of that part of the city. An interesting character, Mr. Jenkins, had at that time charge of the work. He was a baldheaded gentleman and Mr. Ober used to delight in telling the following story: "We have a basement to the mission and there is a trap door which leads up from the lower part to the platform. Mr. Jenkins used to ascend by the stairs, so that the audience saw first a part of his head before he fully appeared. One day he was late for the service and a visiting brother was reading the Scripture lesson. It happened to be the record of the young men who mocked Elisha. And just as the preacher read dramatically, 'Go up thou bald-head! Go up thou bald-head!' Jenkins' bald head popped up, much to the merriment of the audience."

The Baltimore Port Mission has done, and I believe is still doing, a phenomenal work. There is one of the finest Sunday-Schools in the State carried on strictly on Gospel lines. When I was connected through the ministry with the Port Mission, there were some splendid young men who helped in the Gospel work of the Mission. I mention one especially, Mr. Leroy Haslup, now with the Lord. The Mission also maintained a launch, bringing sailors from different vessels to attend the Gospel services. How I did enjoy these Sunday night services, preaching the simple Gospel to these sea-faring men! And what blessed results there were. Sometimes I preached to them in German, for often sailors came from German ships.

Another branch of the work was the Gospel-wagon testimony. Many Sunday afternoons during the summer months for about ten years I went on one of these wagons. A narrow alley was selected, or a public square. Then followed a song led either by a small melodeon or a cornet, or both. A crowd soon gathered. Windows everywhere were crowded with white and colored people. I gave a brief message and New Testaments and Gospel leaflets were distributed. Frequently we drove to German sections, and I preached the Gospel in that language. A number of times I addressed immense Jewish crowds in South Baltimore; at one time over a thousand were gathered and hundreds of copies of *Joseph and His Brethren* were handed out.

One afternoon in 1909 Mr. Gustavus Ober asked me to come with him and inspect a building located on Charles Street. It was the former Baltimore Club Building. We went through the several stories and saw the reception hall, billiard rooms, living rooms, etc. It was a splendid and very well equipped building. Then my friend surprised me by saying, "I bought this building this week, and do you not think it would be a very ideal place for a Bible Institute?" I said, "Yes, with a few alterations it would be a wonderful plant." He stated that he had made the purchase with this in mind, for Baltimore, Washington, and the South needed such an institution. He furthermore said that I was to become the Dean of this institution, that I should move to Baltimore, settle down and begin this work, and that he would see to the proper endowment.

I was greatly surprised by this offer and all I could say was, "You must give me a few weeks to think this over and to pray about it." Now, as the reader remembers, Baltimore was my first charge in 1883. I loved Baltimore as my second home, and many times I had wished I might have my residence there. I had made many friends, and I knew I should be happy there, besides having the honor of beginning such a work and being its head.

But when I waited on the Lord and prayed for His guidance, gradually the conviction came to me that I could not accept the offer of my friend. More than once the still small voice whispered, "Take heed to the ministry which thou hast received in the Lord, that thou fulfil it." The Lord had called me to a nation-wide ministry. He had not cancelled my commission. And so, after waiting on Him, it became clear that I must not turn aside from the unique ministry I had received. Humanly speaking, if I had accepted this call, the great ministry of over twenty-one years, from 1909 to 1930, would not have been possible. Subsequent developments proved that my refusal was according to His will. Mr. Ober sold the building later. But we had a number of meetings there to which the young society folks had been specially invited.

Mr. Ober had a charming summer estate in Lutherville with a beautiful home on a hill top, some ten miles from the city. Many happy Lord's Day mornings were spent there by me in fellowship with Mr. and Mrs. Ober and their most interesting family of nine children. Nor is this all the work done in Baltimore. I held frequently Bible Conferences in the Green Street and Franklin Street Presbyterian and Brown Memorial Churches, and later in the North-minster Church and in other churches. Once eleven Methodist Protestant Churches combined and we had splendid services.

CHAPTER X

I LOVE the Southern States and the Southern people. The first time I came in touch with the good people of the Southland, coming from the North, I felt as if I had entered a new country. The spirit of chivalry is most prominent and everywhere among all classes one finds real gentlemen. Their hospitality and kindness is most refreshing. In religious matters conservatism has ruled, though now the increasing waves of modernism are spreading rapidly through the South and every other portion of the land. Needless to say I made many friends among the folks of the South.

Leaving Baltimore we come to our national Capital *Washington*. Here I ministered in different Presbyterian and Baptist Churches, as well as in the Y. M. C. A. In 1924 I held a splendid Conference for a week in the historic New York Avenue Presbyterian Church, where Abraham Lincoln and other Presidents used to worship. This conference had been arranged by the Hon. John E. Milholland, with whom I had formed an intimate friendship. A number of Senators and Congressmen presided at the different services to introduce me. One of them, Congressman Nelson, said: "Some twelve years ago when I first came to

Washington as a representative I walked through
the Library of Congress and in the magazine section I picked up a small monthly called *Our
Hope.*" He described how he read a good part
of it and then asked the Librarian in case they had
other books by A. C. Gaebelein to send them
over to his chamber in the House of Representa-
tives. Finally a boy came with two armfulls
of books, many of which the Congressman read
from cover to cover. He became a reader of the
magazine and a close student of the Word, and
told the audience what a blessing the magazine
and the books had been to him.

For some reason it never pleased the Lord to
give me much ministry in the State of *Virginia.*
I had invitations and calls to Richmond and other
cities, but could not accept them. In 1910 I
accepted a call to come for a week to *Warrenton,
Va.* The meetings were to be held in the St.
James Episcopal Church, which General Washington used to attend, an historic old building. I
arrived on Saturday. When I was about to
retire, the fire alarm sounded. A big fire had
started, and inasmuch as there was no water
available, it soon was a conflagration. I watched
the spreading flames and to my great sorrow
noticed how the wooden steeple of St. James began
to smoke, and finally it burst into flames and soon
the building was destroyed. The Union meetings
were then held in the next largest building, the

Methodist Episcopal, and there was a splendid attendance and great blessing.

In *North Carolina* I enjoyed a good series of meetings in *Charlotte*, which had been arranged by a young newspaper man, Howard A. Banks, who later became connected with *The Sunday School Times*. *Asheville* was visited twice and successful meetings were held in the Y. M. C. A. and in one of the Baptist churches. On one Sunday morning service one of the deacons after my sermon asked excitedly, "Are you a Baptist?" As I answered him negatively, he became more excited and fairly shouted, "Why are you not a Baptist? Why are you not a Baptist? You preach Baptist doctrine; it is Baptist doctrine you preach!" I quieted him by saying, "You see I preach the Bible, and all true Baptists believe the Bible as I do."

A good deal of work was done by me in the first decade of the Twentieth Century in *Georgia*. I held meetings in *Jackson*, *Macon*, *Augusta*, *Quitman*, *Atlanta*, and in *Savannah*.

Savannah I paid six annual visits. Meetings were held in the Lawton Memorial, the Southside Baptist Church, in a rented hall, and in the Seamen's Bethel. Here as elsewhere there was a small company of people who loved the Word and loved His appearing. What a joy it was to minister to their need and to see others brought to a saving knowledge of Christ! Amongst these was a very aged man.

Strange things happen sometimes in such a ministry. Preaching in one of the Savannah churches on Sunday morning, I selected for a text the parable of the leaven in Matthew xiii. No sooner had I announced the text than the people seemed to be amused, and as I unfolded the text, some smiled and others nodded to each other. I could not understand the meaning of it at all. When I finished, the pastor seemed to be very much agitated and disturbed; he hardly spoke to me. But the whole mystery was solved when a member of that church informed me that the pastor had preached on the same text the previous Sunday. The member added, "You answered all his arguments, for he said leaven is the Gospel and the Gospel leaven is converting the world." But the preacher believed that some one had requested that sermon. Had I known that he had preached on that parable the week before, I would certainly not have chosen it for my text.

In *Tennessee, Chattanooga* was visited many times, the first time in 1897. J. J. Frater, who later became a physician, and Major and Mrs. Mitchell sent the first invitations. Here I met "the grand old man of Chattanooga," Dr. Bachman, the pastor of the large First Presbyterian Church, where I often preached. Conferences were held by me in various Presbyterian and Baptist Churches and also in halls. During my last visit many people told me that they had received their first light through my first visits, and the younger generation assured me that as far as they could remember *Our Hope* had been in the different homes, and that through the reading of it they were led out into the truth. *Knoxville* was visited twice and good conferences held in the First Presbyterian Church and the Library Hall. *Sweetwater, Cleveland, Athens,* in the same state were visited as well as *Memphis.* In *Mississippi* I ministered the truth in *Kosciusko* and *Durant.*

Twice I was a speaker at the *Crescent City, Florida, Conferences.* Two Bible Conferences were held in one of the Baptist Churches and the Opera House of *Orlando.* Later I had a good week's ministry in *Miami Beach.* Alas! the many other places in this State and throughout the Southland which sent calls, but which could not be visited. *Kentucky* was not forgotten with ministry in *Louisville, Bowling Green* and *Ownsboro.* From the latter place I received a very pressing invitation from a leading church and strange to say the request was that I should preach the whole week on nothing but the second coming of our Lord. I hardly could consent to this, for I do not consider the over-emphasis of any Bible doctrine normal. When I arrived at my destination, the pastor took me into his fine study. On a table were a score or more books. He informed me that he had read all these books on prophecy (including the pernicious perversions of Pastor Russell's writings). Then he thought he had mastered the subject and preached a series of sermons. He declared that he had confused himself and his hearers. He wanted me to get them out of the mess and get the real Bible Truth of our Lord's return. Under His blessing I succeeded.

Numerous visits have been made by me to *Baton Rouge, Louisiana.* These visits have done much good, but they would not have been possible without the help of Mr. and Mrs. Amos K. Gordon. Mrs. Gordon for years has been very active in Bible class work and also in circulating the right kind of literature, and through this work has brought a blessing to many. My first conference was held in the First Methodist Church South. The attendance was good from the beginning. On Monday Governor Pleasant came with his wife and attended every service; both were much pleased and helped, and the fact that the Governor of the State thought it worth the while to attend brought in big audiences. My later visits were made in connection with the First Presbyterian Church South. *New Orleans* invited me twice for conferences, and once I visited *Shreveport.*

What a joy it is to find "bread cast upon the waters after many days!" How refreshing and encouraging to find friends from the Southland in Northern and Western States and hear from their lips, "You know, I heard you in Chattanooga and it was the real beginning of my Christian life." Or we remember some who had wandered away and had been restored through the ministry given in another Southern City. But what am I, or who am I, that I should boast of any results He has been pleased to give? It is all of Him, and to Him be the glory!

CHAPTER XI

THE FIRST five years of the twentieth century proved that the vision of ministry I had in 1899 was not an idle dream. Every year additional seals of His gracious approval were given, and soon the scenes of my ministry extended from New England to California and from Manitoba to the border of Mexico. My friends who urged caution, or predicted defeat, acknowledged readily the success of what some called an experiement. Dr. Scofield said to a well-known New York business man: "For years we have talked about a nation-wide ministry in which dispensational truths should be made prominent, a ministry which should reach the members of the true Church in the different denominations. None of us knew how it could be done, and suddenly the Lord raised up this brother to do this very thing." Dr. W. J. Erdman, instead of discouraging me, as he did in the beginning, now gave me words of cheer. The last time I saw him in his eighty-ninth year in front of the building of *The Sunday School Times* in Philadelphia, he said in his terse way, "What a great ministry you have in reaching thousands and magnifying the Lord Jesus Christ!" Dr. Arthur T. Pierson not only approved of this ministry, but frequently we were together in Bible Conferences here and there.

I have often been asked if I like traveling up and down the land, going from North to South, from East to West, living in hotels of all classes and often in farm houses or shacks. I answer with a very positive, "No!" My wife and I always had a comfortable home. I love home-life more than anything. If I had followed my natural inclinations, I would have remained at home, continued in select studies, and indulged my literary disposition. But I followed the command of Romans xii: "Present your bodies a living sacrifice," and that meant giving up myself. Can this be done without cost, or without feeling that sacrifice is indeed sacrifice, though it be a willing sacrifice? Our Lord felt His sacrifice, and so surely shall we, if we are obedient to Him. How well I remember a lesson which came to me in the far Northwest. I had gone to a small settlement in North Dakota. My stopping place was a very small and rather primitive farm-house. The bed was hard and the fare almost insufficient. I thought of home and the children, and said to myself, "Why did I leave my good and comfortable home to come out here for the sake of a handful of people?" I was so homesick that I was tempted to take the next train back. That evening a voice seemed to speak to me in prayer. It must have been His voice. "I left a better home than you could ever leave; I had not where to lay my head; I suffered and died for you." I bowed my head in shame and wept and thanked Him for the little sacrifice I could bring and for the grace which permitted me to seek out some of His beloved sheep and minister to their need. Nor must I forget what all these years of my wandering ministry meant to her, who stood by me so faithfully. Many months each year she spent in a sacrificial widowhood.

In my account of my service for Him I have covered the Eastern States and the Southland in many places, and it may now be in order to turn Northward to *Eastern Canada.* I visited *Toronto* the first time in 1897. Pastor Salmon had invited me for a few meetings, and the first man he introduced me to was one of his church officers by the name of Trout. Salmon—Trout, true Canadian! My regular visits began with 1900 and continued till 1914. The man who backed my ministry, made all preparations, supported the ministry constantly was Stephen H. Chapman. I also mention Robert Kilgour and C. Gszowski who were vitally interested in my ministry. Mr. Chapman belonged to the Brethren. They had a small hall. My frequent visits proved a great blessing to this assembly. Under the leadership of Mr. Chapman a nice building was erected, and on my suggestion it was called "Maranatha Hall." I held the first meetings there, and had many conferences. One of the blessed sights in these services was to see Dr. J. B. Parsons, for many years pastor of Knox Church, in the front seat in every service with his Bible in his hands. He was one of the Niagara brethren, and a venerable looking saint with a long white beard.

But greater ministry opened for me in Toronto. The brethren mentioned above, Chapman, Gszowski and Kilgour, rented Zion Congregational Church on College Street for a week at a time and great audiences, filling the big auditorium, gathered. Those were days of blessing. Many suggested that I move to Canada, and several wealthy brethren offered to purchase Zion Church and turn it over to me. But my commission was not to become a pastor, but to minister to the flock of God. Similar offers came to me from time to time, several times from very influential churches. But I remembered the Spirit's advice given through Paul, "Say to Archippus, Take heed to the ministry which thou hast received in the Lord, that thou fulfill it" (Col. iv:17).

Besides holding numerous Bible conferences in Zion Church, I preached many times in the Yonge Street Mission. Happy, shouting Davies was the leader, and we had great crowds. There were many instances of real salvation. Several conferences were held in the Y. M. C. A. Hall by Dr. Scofield and me. This hall had the reputation of being infested with many mice. One evening while giving an address on a most solemn theme, I became conscious that I was losing the attention of some in the great audience. They were watching a mouse, which sat beside the pulpit, manifesting such attention that it appeared as if the creature were following the discourse. I stepped a little nearer and stamped with my foot. It disappeared and I thought my trouble was ended. But after a few minutes a lady in the audience gave a terrifying shriek, at the same time holding her skirts. Enough said! I had hard work to restore the equilibrium of my hearers. A number of Presbyterian and Baptist churches welcomed me for a week's meetings, among the latter the Walmer Road Baptist Church, Elmore Harris, Pastor. He was a fine Christian gentleman, and we had much fellowship together. He had founded the Toronto Bible Training School on College Street and given for its headquarters a fine building. He inaugurated monthly meetings for a lecture on our Lord's return, and I was one of the first whom he invited to give this lecture. I did so for eight years, giving a lecture each year. My visits to Toronto of late have almost ceased, with the exception of two yearly visits to supply the Knox Presbyterian Church and hold several Bible conferences.

In *Hamilton* six conferences were held, two in the Gospel Tabernacle and the others in different churches and halls. Dr. Arthur T. Pierson spent a week with me in one of these

conferences. *Brantford* had my ministry for some
six years with yearly conferences in Bethel and
Victoria halls and one of the Baptist churches.
Then visits were made to *Oshawa* and *Peterboro*, to
Galt, Guelph and *Berlin*, now called *Kitchener*. In
one of the Scotch Presbyterian churches, the pastor
had introduced musical programs for Sunday
evenings, much to the disgust of the good old
Scotch folks, who would have rather heard a good
sermon. The evening I was to preach he had his
musical performance, and when it got to be 8:45
he turned to me and said, "When this piece is
finished you preach, but remember the people
want to be out sharp at nine." I made a mental
remark to myself, "They surely will not get out at
nine tonight." So I preached a Gospel sermon
which lasted just an hour. Oh! how these Scotch
friends thanked me and even the Pastor said:
"It was good, but a wee little bit too long." In
1908 I held a successful conference in *Tilsonburg*.

In *St. Thomas* I held a week's meetings. On
Sunday night after I had preached the Gospel to a
full house in the Baptist Church, the pastor tried to
make the people accept the message. There was
no response. My theory that, if the Gospel is
faithfully preached, the Lord will take care of it
was vindicated a year later. A Toronto business
man told me he met a section hand of the Michigan
Central Railroad on a train. He sat alongside of
him, and when my friend opened his satchel and

took out *Our Hope*, the man became interested and wanted to see the first page. "Oh! he burst out, I saw this magazine before and I know the man. Last year he preached in St. Thomas when we were suddenly laid off and I went to church. Mr. Gaebelein preached, and when he told us about the plan of salvation from John v:24, I accepted Christ and was saved."

Perth and *Kingston* had each a good visit with much blessing. In 1904 I gave six addresses before the Frontier Sunday School Association in the Methodist Church of *Huntington*, Province of *Quebec*. The City of *Quebec* was visited three times and also *Montreal*.

The greater work in Western Canada we shall reach later.

CHAPTER XII

ONE OF the delightful experiences in this ministry is the way my Lord and Master led forward. He Himself went before and opened doors and hearts. To me it seems a very poor testimony for men to advertise themselves and offer their services on "reasonable terms." I never needed to do this. The Lord took care of all, and many, many times I saw His loving hand in opening doors and supplying every need. Of late years my prayer has been, and is, to be still more guided by Him. Nor did I accept every call as it came. I found it the very best policy to wait on Him in prayer and to ask, "Lord, what wilt Thou have me to do?" Such dependence is well pleasing in His sight. Big denominational and interdenominational conferences and movements had not much use for me. I should have liked to speak to gathered thousands the message the Lord has given me, but when I was ignored I took it as from Him. Yet the Lord many times gave me thousands to speak to, and for a number of years I reached under His guidance larger numbers of God's people than almost any other Bible teacher or preacher in this country.

We could now pass on from state to state, city to city, town to town, and hamlet to hamlet across

the country. But I can confine myself only to
some of the outstanding places of the different
states, for the great Northwest, the charming
Southwest and the entire Pacific Coast, will bring
to light many and most blessed experiences in
this glorious service.

In *Ohio* my first visit was made in 1894 to
Cincinnati. For almost ten years I held yearly
meetings in *Dayton*, Ohio. A beloved physician,
now with the Lord, Dr. Ensey, had a Bible class,
and he was used in opening the door to different
churches. I was not a stranger in Dayton, for
in 1897 Professor Morehead and myself had addressed large meetings in the Y. M. C. A. Other
conferences were held in different United Brethren, Baptist and Methodist churches and several
with Peter Quartel of the City Mission. There
are many people in Dayton who were led out into
the Truth by my visits. I also addressed a great
meeting in the Community Hall.

I shall mention briefly various visits to *Cleveland*,
Columbus, *Archbold*, *Akron*, *Mansfield*, *Sandusky*,
Lima and *Portsmouth.* A great conference was
held in the latter place, which resulted in much
blessing. And besides these larger cities, small
places were visited, not because large audiences
awaited me, but because it was His will, and I
always had a special blessing when I turned to
small towns or villages. Frequently people won-

dered that I should visit small places, where no financial support could be expected.

In *Michigan* the most visits were made to *Detroit*. My first conference was held in the Central Presbyterian Church, where Marcus Scott was pastor. Dr. Scofield and I held a conference there, and years later I paid yearly visits to the same church when C. R. Scafe was pastor. Also numerous conferences, sometimes thrice and four times a year, were held in Salem Hall. Mr. John Mouat, a friend of Malachi Taylor, Sinclair Harcus, and Fred. M. Leach were the leading brethren, and many times the hall was crowded. Five conferences were held by me in *Adrian*. A travelling man, Mr. W. A. Hoisington, had been frequently in New York, and then always came to the noon-day meetings in Temple Court, where we met. Through him a goodly company of believers were gathered in this Michigan town, and now they have their own building and a thriving Sunday School and Assembly. Conferences were held in *Pontiac* and several smaller towns, also in *Traverse City, Grand Rapids, Battle Creek* and *Muskegon*. In Muskegon is a strong Holland Church under the leadership of my friend, H. Bultema. He was put out of the Christian Reformed Church, because he preached the premillennial Coming of the Lord. As a result of this unscriptural action, the First Berean Church was started, and the Lord's blessing has rested richly

upon the ministry of this good brother. One
week was spent some nine years ago at *Gull Lake*
Summer Conference. For several years the conference leaders have urged me to take a continued
and more prominent part in the development of
Gull Lake, but it has been out of my reach.

Fort Wayne and *South Bend* in *Indiana* were
visited. Without touching on every city, town and
village where I ministered the Word of God,
I refer next to *Chicago*. My first visit to the
Moody Church was in 1898. One evening, or
perhaps it was during the afternoon, Professor
Morehead, who was giving lectures to the students,
came in. I was talking on the Book of Jonah and
explained that Jonah was not only a type of our
Lord, but a type of Israel. I unfolded this type
as I have done in my book on *The Jewish Question*, and I see yet this beloved brother eagerly
drinking it in, and when I had finished he had
glowing words of appreciation. A few years
later when Dr. James M. Gray became Dean of
the Institute I made many visits to Chicago,
teaching frequently for two and three weeks the
entire student body. There was rich fruit from
this ministry. I have found preachers in different
parts of the country who told me that my ministry helped them to get established in the truth
and not a few, who had gone to the Institute without any definite plans, decided then to give their
lives to the ministry of the Gospel. When the

Moody Church was without a pastor, I frequently supplied the pulpit and preached in many other churches of the city.

As already stated, I took the first steps in planning a Prophetic Conference in Chicago in the early part of 1914. It was a great conference and large audiences gathered in every service. It was also a significant conference, for a few months later the world war started. The testimony given was clear-cut and every phase of the premillennial Coming of our Lord and kindred themes was fully dealt with. I spoke on the Future of Israel and gave another address on the Apostasy of Christendom. Several of the prominent speakers, R. McWatty Russell, W. H. Griffith Thomas and C. I. Scofield, have since gone to be with the Lord.

I shall not follow the many other visits to Chicago but shall speak of several visits to *Oak Park*. My conferences there were held in the First Methodist Church; both were rich in blessing. A certain modernistic preacher seemed to oppose the efforts which were made. His congregation erected a new church building. While under construction the workmen had put up a big sign in the doorway—*Danger! Keep out!* I used it effectually as an illustration and said that all churches in which the faith is denied ought to have such a sign to warn the people. Two very successful Conferences were held with our Swedish Brethren in *Rockford*.

Numerous smaller towns visited by me in Illinois included *Jerseyville, Springfield, Bayliss, Belleville, Edwardsville, Alton, Granite City, Peoria, Pekin, Groveland, Morton,* and others.

My first visit to *Missouri* was made in 1896, for it was in this year that I first came to *St. Louis.* During the time of my activity among the Jewish people, a branch of the Hope of Israel had been opened in this city. Mrs. C. D. Ely was instrumental in bringing this about. She rented an old church building on Morgan Street, and for several years I made almost monthly visits to St. Louis, speaking to Jews and Gentiles. Dr. James H. Brookes was still living, and he had a very warm heart for any effort to give the Gospel to the Jews. Two conferences were held in St. Louis in 1897 and 1898. One was held in the Morgan Street Church. The speakers were Reuben A. Torrey, W. J. Erdman, Nathanael West, and I. I roomed with Dr. West, but it was a sleepless night; only towards five in the morning did I get some rest. Dr. West was a great scholar and strong advocate of the premillennial coming of our Lord. But we differed on the church and the great tribulation.

Unlike Brookes, Gordon, Parsons, Needham myself and others, Dr. West believed that the church would be on earth till the very end of that period of trouble. He tried hard to win me over to his side, and started in about 11 P.M. with the ninth chapter of Daniel, verses 25-27. After we had gone over the Hebrew text and agreed on the correct translation, he attempted to build his argument on this prophecy, but failed to gain his point. Then we drifted to the second chapter of the second Epistle to the Thessalonians and here we kept our vigil. West maintained that the hindering power is human government; I said that it is the Holy Spirit. It was a hot conflict which strengthened greatly my belief in my view, which I believe is based on Scripture. We were good friends. The last time I met Dr. West left a blessed memory with me. He had written me a very sharp, almost ungracious letter. I met him in the old Grand Central Station in New York. He took me by the hand and with tears in his eyes he said, "I am afraid, brother Gaebelein, I have done you a wrong; please forgive me." This was the last time we met.

The other conference was held in Dr. Brookes's church a year after he was called home. The speakers were Dr. Torrey, Prof. Morehead, George Needham, Elmore Harris, and I. I also preached in numerous German churches. While preaching in a certain Church on a Lord's day morning, a heavy wind came up, and as the church was crowded with people, the thought came to me, "What if one of these western tornadoes should strike us now?" A week later the disastrous tornado struck St. Louis which destroyed so many human lives, and three weeks later in viewing the ruins in South St. Louis I saw just one corner of the church standing where I had preached. But my real work in St. Louis began with 1901. In this year I met for the first time another noble member of the family of God, John B. Buss. It did not take us long to become close friends. He welcomed me to his home in *Jennings, Mo.*, and here in fellowship with him and his interesting family I spent many weeks till his home-call some twelve years later. Conferences were held first in a chapel, and later Mr. Buss built a beautiful Bible Hall on Finney Avenue, where I held many conferences. During the St. Louis World-Fair in 1904 we held a big conference in the Y. M. C. A. on Grand Avenue. The speakers were Dr. C. I. Scofield, F. C. Jennings, John M. Carnie, and I. Another conference was held by Dr. Scofield and myself in the First Congregational Church. From 1915 to 1925 I held yearly conferences in Dr. Brookes' old church at Washington Ave. and Compton Street. I was privileged to hold the last conference in this historic building before the congregation moved to their new church home on Wydown Boulevard, and it was my privilege to hold the first Bible Conferences in the Memorial Church.

Other places in Missouri where I ministered are *Jefferson City, Carrolton* and *Springfield, St. Joseph, Neosho,* and *Kansas City*. Kansas City I visited the first time in 1897, when I spoke in a Gospel

Mission. Six other visits were made, and conferences held in several Baptist and Presbyterian Churches and in a Bible Hall.

As I follow my tracks, it fills my heart with praise and thanksgiving to Him who made all this work possible, who gave the strength and the courage, kept me from accident and harm, and used me in bringing blessing, comfort, and hope to the hearts and homes of so many people and also in leading so many to Himself as their Saviour.

Going northward we come to the state of *Iowa*. *Council Bluffs* was visited regularly for a number of years. Mr. A. E. Morehouse had sent the first call and I had preached a week on each visit in different churches. One interesting guidance showing how the Lord protects his servant I must mention. It has been my custom in Western States never to carry large sums of money on my person on account of the many hold-ups. I generally locked my money in my suitcase. One noon when I left the home of Mr. Morehouse to go to the early afternoon meeting, I was compelled to turn back, and I took all my money to carry it along to the meeting, hardly knowing why I did this. After the meeting I visited the shop of Mr. Morehouse, and there came a telephone message for Mr. Morehouse to come home at once. When we arrived we found that during our absence in the meeting a burglar had entered and ransacked the whole house. He had broken open my suit case and scattered the contents all over the room. The Lord had taken care of me.

Near Council Bluffs is *Omaha, Nebraska,* and here too the Lord permitted me to minister a number of times. Other places in Iowa where I preached are *Waterloo* where several conferences were held as well as in *Harlan, Muscatine, Aplington, Parkersburg* and *Pella.* The last-named town was visited a number of time. The inhabitants are mostly all Hollanders, and they received the word with gladness.

I also mention a small village where I had a great blessing—*Grandview.* Here I was lodged in a very small farm house a good distance from the railroad station. Seeking an early rest I was disturbed by a rustling noise and discovered that it was made by mice, which went through my coat pocket where I had carried my lunch. After a while I felt them on the bed covering. I did not know what to do, but finally I invented a new mousetrap. I put a porcelain basin, half full with water on the floor and blew out the candle to see what would happen. It did not take long till I heard a splash, and then another, and another, and soon I had dead mice. But what was the blessing I received? Certainly not the mice. On the next morning when the dear old saint, a poor farmer, asked me to come to a simple breakfast, and while we were eating, I heard an unearthly shriek. The farmer went to the stairs which led to the attic and after a while he brought down a young man about thirty years of age. He was an imbecile, with staring eyes and half-open mouth covered with saliva. When he was two years old some terrible brain disease, perhaps meningitis, had wrecked this young life and left him in this awful state. Then I watched the father. How patiently he dealt with him! He washed him, spoke soothingly to the boy, while the boy looked at him as a satisfied animal would look. He combed his hair, he prepared his food, he took the spoon and fed him. He undressed him at night. Year after year, month after month, week after week, and day by day the aged father had done this. Then I said to myself, if an earthly father can manifest such love, such kindness, such patience, what must be the infinite love of our heavenly Father? In that lonely, uncomfortable farm house, I received a vision of the love of God our Father such as I had never had before.

CHAPTER XIII

WHEN Jude, the servant of Christ, took his pen to write a letter to the Christians of his day, he had it upon his heart to write about the common salvation, which is the Gospel. But when it came to the execution of this purpose the power which guided his pen constrained him to exhort the Christians to contend earnestly for the faith once and for all delivered to the Saints. There is a lesson here. As all Bible students know, the little Epistle of Jude has a special meaning for these last days. Like Jude we must love the Gospel, as the nearest and dearest truth to our hearts, and besides the Gospel it is our solemn duty in these days of falling away to contend earnestly for the faith. *Our Hope* has been specially used in this direction, so that it is now looked upon as the most conservative magazine published, which has courage enough to speak out without any compromise. Year after year the inventions of rationalistic professing Christians have been laid bare, and monthly warnings have been sounded by my pen as to the encroaching apostasy. What I foresaw in connection with the Methodist denomination came true, and the falling away, predicted in the New Testament, is now going on in nearly all the Protestant denominations. I also have received literally hundreds of letters during the last twenty-five years from persons who had followed some of the swamp-lights of our times, different delusive systems, and through my warnings and exposures had been graciously delivered. This is still a part of the ministry of the magazine. When the Pentecostal-Gift of Tongue delusion first came up in 1906, even good men thought it might be a new manifestation of the Spirit. I tested it by the Word of God, and at once said, "It is spurious. It is not of God! It is like the Irvingite movement of Satanic counterfeit!" I did not hesitate to publish this verdict. And so one day a letter came from one of the first Pentecostalite assemblies in California, that they were praying together that the Lord strike me dead for having written that the whole thing is of Satan!

But it is not an easy work to warn, to expose, to call black—black, and white—white. It does not make a man popular. Even good Christians think one should not be so harsh and call those who deny our holy Lord as the Virgin-born Son of God and who disbelieve the physical resurrection, infidels and enemies of the Gospel. According to some they ought to be handled tenderly with nice, soft kid-gloves.

A cultured Christian lady exhorted me once to be a little more like John, lovely, loving John. I answered her that this was my great ambition to be like John—to love Him who first loved us, to

love the brethren, to love every member of the
family of God, and to be like John and say, "Who
is a liar but he that denieth that Jesus is the Christ?"
(1 Jno. ii:22) John is the Apostle of love, but he is
also Bonarges, a son of thunder. Yes, I think I
could have been much more popular and have
succeeded better in wordly attainments, if I had
not been quite so loyal to the truth of God. So
I have heard hard speeches against me, but they
were sweet after all, for they were "for Christ's
sake." Outside of the camp we must needs bear
His reproach. I know something of that.

In 1901 and 1902 *Our Hope* almost doubled its
subscription list. It came about in a strange way.
A certain magazine, which no longer exists and
whose Editor is also gone home, so that I do not
care to mention either, attacked my testimony on
prophetic lines. Everything was done to belittle
my efforts. A whole issue was devoted to dis-
credit me in every way. I kept silent and did a
lot of praying those days, and at the same time I
continued to teach the truth through my pages.

Then letters came from everywhere. They
wanted sample copies of that paper they had read
about. Others admired the Christian spirit in not
answering back. One brother wrote that he subscribed for the other magazine not alone for himself, but for thirty other friends, and he transferred
the whole list to me. About two thousand new
subscribers came to me in this way.

The greatest of all servants of Christ, Paul, who delighted to call himself the slave of Christ, wrote among other things these words, "By honour and dishonour, by evil report and good report". (2 Cor. vi:8) The true servant of the Lord may well expect the slandering, maligning tongue. But how is he to behave then?

For about two years in the beginning of our century I was conscious that somebody was circulating falsehoods about myself and the work I was doing. All kinds of insinuations must have been made. Without hearing anything definite, I felt that an enemy was at work in different parts of the country. Some people seemed to begin to mistrust me. I did not lose any sleep over it, for I knew that such evil reports, backbitings, and slanders could not hurt me in the least. It was all in the hands of the Lord whom I serve.

On a certain day I had a visitor. He was almost in rags. As he saw me, he began to weep hysterically and tried to cast himself at my feet. Then when he had become quiet he said, "I am S. G. I met you some years ago and I took a great dislike to you. Yes, I have hated you bitterly, I do not know why. But I have gone about and lied about you, slandered you." Then he began to sob again and said, "See what God has done to me! See what God has done to me! Forgive me before I die!" He was half dead. I saw to it that he was taken to a good hospital, where he passed away five weeks later.

Oh! Christian servant, you need not defend yourself against wrong accusations. Your Lord is
sufficient! Put it into His hands! and if you have
done wrong confess to Him and put all your
failures into His hands.

But we must resume our travels and reach the
state of *Minnesota* next, going north from Iowa.
I visited the twin cities *Minneapolis—St. Paul* the
first time in 1897, and my first addresses were given
in a Gospel Mission in St. Paul. On Lord's day I
spoke for the first time in the First Baptist Church
of Minneapolis. I believe Dr. W. B. Riley had then
been in the pastorate of this church only a short
time. In the afternoon I addressed a good meeting
in the Y. M. C. A. It was an interesting occasion.
My topic was "The Book of Jonah". On Saturday
a reporter of the *Minneapolis Journal* had called
on me with a message from the Editor. He informed me that Dr. Lyman Abbott from Brooklyn
was to preach on Sunday morning in Plymouth
Church, and that he would give the sermon on
"Jonah and the Whale" which had stirred up the
people in Brooklyn. He suggested that I take the
same theme and present it in the orthodox way,
and the promise was made that a reporter should
attend each meeting and that reports of the two
addresses were to be printed on Monday morning.
I had the advantage over Dr. Lyman Abbott, for
he knew nothing of what was going on. On Monday
morning a full newspaper page brought the two

addresses. Over Dr. Abbott's sermon the reporter put *Liberal* and over mine the word *Literal*.

Just a word about Dr. Lyman Abbott's sermon. It had been preached in Brooklyn. In it the whole book of Jonah had been treated as a book of fiction with no historical background, the view being taken that it was unreliable and could not be a prophecy concerning Christ. Then Dr. Abbott started on a tour over the country and that "famous" sermon was demanded everywhere. But more—then Dr. Lyman Abbott began to slide back into all kinds of errors, until finally nearly everything of essential Christianity was given up by him.

In 1905 and 1906 I returned to Minneapolis where, besides meetings in the First Baptist Church, Dr. Riley had arranged conferences on the Minnesota State Fair Grounds midway between Minneapolis and St. Paul. We had immense crowds in one of the halls. One evening, while several thousand were gathered, I preached on "His Riches." Afterwards I heard of most gracious results from this service. In 1906 aged Dr. Grattan Guinness of London was one of the other speakers, but our interpretation of prophecy did not go together, for he did not believe in the futurist interpretation of the book of Revelation. I also preached in Westminster Presbyterian Church, in the Bethlehem Presbyterian Church, in several Methodist Churches, and later held conferences in the Stewart Memorial and in the Swedish Tabernacle.

About ten years ago I met for the first time in Minneapolis Mr. Hershel V. Jones the Editor of the *Minneapolis Journal,* the outstanding newspaper of the Northwest. As I walked into his office and introduced myself, I received a most hearty welcome. I dined with him in his beautiful home and he told me what a great blessing *Our Hope* had been to him. While he was in San Diego, a number of years before, a friend told him that he had subscribed to the magazine for him. After reading it for a year, Mr. Jones said that his religious thinking had been completely revolutionized; he had found things in the Bible he never dreamt were there. Pointing to an armchair in his library he said, "This is my choicest spot early Sunday morning. I sit here with *Our Hope* and my Bible and have sweet communion." He read nearly all my books. He was a great lover of very old and rare books and manuscripts and a great collector. In fact he left a library worth several million dollars. He helped the Stony Brook School liberally and left twenty thousand dollars in his will for the School. What blessing his friend started when he sent Mr. Jones *Our Hope*!

In *St. Paul* I have held many yearly conferences under the leadership of Peter McFarlane in the Union Gospel Mission, which have been very well attended and have brought great blessing to young and old. I also ministered in other churches, among them the Dayton Ave. and House of Hope Presbyterian Churches.

South of the Twin Cities is *Faribault*. Here I spent in several yearly visits profitable weeks with Mr. and Mrs. Archer Young, who were instrumental in securing a ministry for me there. A conference was held in *Northfield* and later in *Mountain Lake* with the German Mennonite brethren.

Northward I visited many towns and villages for years. How I wish I could rehearse all the incidents and the blessings and also the hardships connected with these visits, as they rise up in my memory!

Duluth has had several conferences held in the First Presbyterian Church and in one of the Baptist churches. Then there were several summer conferences at *Bemidji* on beautiful Lake Bemidji. While these summer conferences, which I addressed during three seasons, were not very large, great good was done through the ministry, especially among the country preachers. At *Staples* a former Congregational preacher named George Hunt had begun an assembly. He had been to Sea Cliff where we had met, and for a number of years before he went to the far Northwest, he did much in evangelizing this region. I spent three seasons with him. I refer also to *Alexandria, Long Prairie, Parker's Prairie, Vincent* and *Crookston*.

Of late years through the financial support of Mr.

BIBLE CONFERENCE IN BEMIDJI, MINNESOTA. MR. GAEBELEIN IS IN THE CENTER AND TO HIS LEFT IS DR. SWEARINGEN, PASTOR OF THE HOUSE OF HOPE CHURCH IN ST. PAUL

Sidney T. Smith in Winnipeg and under his and Peter McFarlane's direction many of the smaller Northern towns have been visited. I spent a week each in the following towns: *Warren, Thief River Falls, Fergus Falls* and *Hallock*. In the latter town I stopped in an old place called "Hotel." On Sunday morning I asked for oatmeal. They had none. I asked for fruit. They were out of it. "What about eggs?" "We did not get any last night." So all I could get was some bread and butter and coffee. But was it coffee? That is the question still. But there were wonderful blessings everywhere. In Warren we had to buy out the moving-picture place to accommodate the crowds from everywhere. In Thief River Falls no church building was large enough; we had to take the community hall. Many were saved, and Christians enlightened and quickened through the ministry of the Word.

In my ministry in *North and South Dakota,* I visited *Fargo, Grand Forks, Langdon, Pembina, Wahpeton, Cooperstown, Marion and Freeman, S.D.*

In all these states the Lord gave great encouragement, as He also did in *Wisconsin.* The places in this state where I ministered the most are *Milwaukee, Racine, Watertown* and *Sheboygan.* Milwaukee was opened through Charles W. Conaway and Mr. Huston. Conferences were held in different churches. Five visits were made to *Racine* and several to *Watertown,* where I held meetings in the Moravian Church in English and German. The meetings in *Sheboygan* were held in a German Reformed Church. I am looking forward to the harvest day. I am confident that this seed sowing, done in faith and much self-denial, has brought much fruit.

CHAPTER XIV

ONE OF the temptations of a busy life of ministry is the neglect of study, and especially of that which is most essential, the study of the Word of God and prayer. Ministry can only be kept fresh by a real growth in the knowledge and grace of our Lord Jesus Christ, and such a growth demands a diligent and prayerful study of the Bible. Now the Bible study of a servant should not be done primarily with the thought of obtaining material for new addresses or sermons. The higher object must be the thought of learning more about Himself—that is, feeding one's own soul. True ministry means to minister Christ, whether it is to saints or sinners. It has been my custom for many years when taking the Bible in hand, to breathe this brief prayer: "Father, by Thy Spirit show me now something about Thy Son; reveal to me afresh His Person and His Glory." I have never prayed thus in vain. And what a joy it is to take what is received through His grace and minister it to others! Ministry which is born in prayer, and which aims to glorify Christ; is the ministry which pleases God and must be effectual. Not that I have always, and unbrokenly, practised this high ideal. How many failures there have

169

been, and how the same lessons had to be learned anew! But He whom we serve is not a harsh master. He still treats us in the same kind and gracious way as He did Peter, and the servant's confession and humiliation leads always to higher service.

Another danger is pride and self-exaltation. Both have led to the ignominious downfall of many a preacher and Bible teacher. I have watched some in their careers. Their aim was not to exalt the Lord whom they served; they put themselves first. They advertised themselves as "one of the world's greatest" and demanded certain financial terms. I have known numerous cases of such who, when the people did not respond financially, upbraided them. Then, in order to be more popular, these men have omitted certain truths, which are unpopular with the masses. It is not hard to guess the spiritual failure which followed. Pride and self-exaltation link the child of God with the being who fell by pride, who exalted himself. The Lord cannot tolerate this in the lives of His children. He has promised more grace to the humble. He tells us to be clothed with humility; He resisteth the proud. The new nature craves humility, as it craves holiness, and if these cravings are not satisfied, the Holy Spirit in us is grieved and cannot manifest His power in life and ministry. The Lord impressed this upon me many years ago. For

almost thirty years, at the close of the year, and
the beginning of the new year, I spent hours in
prayer, and as I read the entries in my journals I
find that the prayer for a deeper humility was the
predominant prayer. It is still so. I believe it
was George Mueller, the great man of faith and
prayer, who prayed as he was getting older,
"Lord save me from becoming a proud, self-
centered old man".

There is a sin which has done untold harm to
the servants of Christ; it is the sin of flattery.
Many times I have said, and written in letters,
that I fear not the slandering, the backbiting
tongue; but the flattering tongue I dread. Rather
slander me than flatter me. "A man that flattereth
his neighbor spreadeth a net for his feet" (Prov.
xxix: 5). "A flattering mouth worketh ruin" (Prov.
xxvi: 28). Flattery feeds pride. The natural man
loves it and only too many servants of Christ
love it, and what is still more despicable, some
flatter those who hold high positions and are wealthy
and influential. And the rich and influential love
to have it so. The servant of Christ who does
this, though he may be orthodox in his belief,
manifests one of the characteristics of the apost-
ates of the last days, as Jude bears witness—
"walking after their own lusts, and their mouths
speaketh great swelling words, having men's
persons in admiration, because of advantage"
(Jude verse 16).

In 1905 I often looked at the map of the North-American continent, and having made several visits to Minnesota, I wondered if the Lord would permit me to enter as His servant into the great Canadian Northwest. As I did all along, praying for guidance, and for open doors, I also prayed earnestly for ministry in Manitoba and the other provinces. This prayer was soon answered. A brother, Mr. James M. Reid, had moved from Toronto to *Winnipeg*, and as he knew of my large ministry in Ontario, and the blessings which had followed, he suggested that I visit the capital of *Manitoba*. This was providential, for just about that time I had met a young Baptist preacher in Minneapolis, who was then the pastor of the Baptist church in *Portage La Prairie*, Manitoba, and he urged me to give him a week's meetings, and so in 1905 I made my first trip to Manitoba. The conference in Portage La Prairie was crowned with much blessing. A second conference was held in the same city several years later in the Christian church, for Mr. Neil Herman, the pastor of the Baptist church, had left the city.

Mr. Reid had obtained the Y. M. C. A. of Winnipeg for my meetings. There was a good congregation present, and I delivered my first address in the city, where for twenty-five years I have ministered annually, and for several years I even made semi-annual visits. After my address two persons came to greet me, among many others, whose words I have not forgotten. The one was a middle-aged Christian, and he seemed to have been anxious to know my views on baptism. The other was a very young man, and as he took my hand and spoke hearty words as to the message, he said, "This settles it for me". He made there and then a noble decision. This young man was Sidney T. Smith. One look into his face convinced me of straightforwardness, and that he was a young man worth-while. I promised that I would pray for him. We were much together during this first visit, and I urged him to study diligently, and to start as soon as possible a Bible class. He was a clerk in his uncle's grain business. And now more than twenty-five years after Sidney T. Smith is the head of one of the largest Grain Companies on this continent, the Reliance Grain Company. The hand of the Lord has rested upon him in great blessing. Better still he has been foremost, and is so still, in Christian work, being the President of the Canadian Bible Society, and the leader and supporter of a most unique work in the city of Winnipeg. But we must follow the development of the work in Winnipeg to learn what God has wrought. First, as I visited Winnipeg again, Manitoba Hall was rented for regular meetings for Bible study. These meetings were continued by Mr Smith and others. On my second visit I supplied for three Lord's days the First Baptist church, which had no pastor. The church had a seating capacity of over 1500. Every service brought capacity houses and one night a hundred or more could not be accommodated. I also held a week's Bible Conference in the same building. This ministry was crowned with great blessing, as I found out later. About eight years after I was on the Pacific coast and found a group of young men who lived formerly in Winnipeg and who were led into the Truth by my ministry in the First Baptist Church.

With my third visit something is connected which I cannot pass by. During all these years of travail as His servant, I have never seen or been in an accident. Some have said, "You lead a charmed life." No! The Master whom I serve is Lord of all. All angels, and powers and principalities are made subject unto Him. If He sends forth His servants, opens the doors for ministry, He also will keep them from evil, and keep them in health and strength. Each time I bought a railroad ticket the agent tried to persuade me to take out an accident policy. I said to many of them, "I do not believe in accidents. The One for whom I work will take care of me". I experienced this on my third visit to Winnipeg. Going north on one of the best roads in the country, the Great Northern, I noticed in the Pullman a number of rather rough looking young men who used vile language and

whose every other word was a curse word. I said
to myself, "Perhaps I am the only Christian
believer on this train." And so, as I sought my
berth, I prayed very earnestly for His protection
during the on-coming night. As I went to sleep, I
noticed a storm was advancing from the Northwest. I slept about as soundly as Peter in the
prison. When I awoke the sun was shining
brightly, and as I looked at my watch I saw we
were about due in Winnipeg. Then we passed a
station and much to my surprise I noticed we
were still in Minnesota, some 230 miles south of
Manitoba. I dressed and asked the brakeman
why we had been delayed almost six hours. He
told me the following story:

> We ran last night into a terrific storm. A cloud-
> burst happened above on our road and one of the
> wooden bridges was completely washed away. Our
> engineer and the train crew knew nothing of it, but
> suddenly we saw a lantern signalling the engineer.
> He slowed up, and when the train came to a full
> stop, we all were horrified to find if we had gone five
> yards more the whole train would have plunged
> into a deep gulch with a raging torrent, and prob-
> ably all on board would have perished. The man
> who flagged the train was a farmer. He had re-
> tired, but claimed to have heard a voice which woke
> him up. When he heard the rushing waters and
> the distant whistle of the train, he quickly lit his
> lantern and stopped the train.

I believe the Lord sent an angel to save me and
all on board. In order to verify this story I
wrote to the officials of the Great Northern in

St. Paul. They confirmed all, and gave me the name and address of the farmer, to whom I sent a nice letter and a copy of *His Riches*. A gentleman, a Christian, to whom I related this experience said to me, "When I read the newspaper account of this escape, I said to myself—'I wonder who was on that train that the Lord did this miracle.'"

My third visit showed that the testimony in Winnipeg had increased, and the Westminster Presbyterian Church was secured in which I held a very successful Bible Conference. I had the same church building in a number of my visits. At one of these I was told that a certain Methodist preacher, Dr. B., was giving a lecture on the first eleven chapters of the Book of Genesis. I think the title of the lecture was "Revelation or Myth?" This gentleman, belonging to the destructive school of Bible criticism, presented his modernistic views on these foundation chapters of the Bible. The lecture was given mostly to young people. The Winnipeg friends asked me if I would give a lecture on the same topic. I was glad for the opportunity to answer these rationalistic conceptions and interpretations. It was well-advertised and the church was full, many college students were in the audience, and Dr. B. appeared in person. In delivering my lecture I showed our orthodox viewpoint and spoke of the fact that the Babylonian and Assyrian mythologies are only faint echoes of the original, primitive revelation, which the whole race had in the beginning. Knowing the arguments of the modernistic school, I took them up one after another under the enthusiastic applause of the young people, many of whom thanked me for the words I had spoken which had strengthened their faith. Said one of the brethren, "But Dr. B. was mad as he left the church; you certainly will hear from him." But I never did.

At another visit I gave a lecture on the Pentecostal-Gift of Tongues delusion, which had invaded Winnipeg and was drawing simple-minded and untaught Christians. They knew, of course, what I would say about this counterfeit movement. When I entered the pulpit I felt greatly depressed. I looked over the great audience and I noticed that many of the deluded adherents of the Pentecostal sect were in the congregation. There seemed to me a strange power in that meeting. I whispered to the brother sitting alongside of me, "Do let us pray; there is an awful antagonism here." When I got up to speak, it seemed as if an unseen hand tried to keep back my words, and while I struggled for expression I cried to the Lord, and all at once there came another power upon me; it was the Holy Spirit. The depression vanished, and the feeling I had disappeared, and I received such a wonderful liberty that I talked rapidly and fluently for a whole hour. While I was speaking, new light came to me on the question, and I saw all over the audience faces which changed from antagonism to approval. When I had concluded many people came and told me that their eyes had been opened. Some were delivered, among them a rector of the Church of England.

Mr. Smith and the other friends interested in the work rented a small chapel on Beverley Street, where the regular meetings were now held. These consisted in a Lord's day morning service, a Sunday School, a Lord's day evening gospel meeting, prayer meeting and a Bible reading during the week. Other teachers were invited to come and to minister, and as the work had outgrown the Beverley Chapel a much larger place was rented, and called Elim Chapel. This place is on the corner of Sherbrooke and Ellice Avenue. The larger place brought larger crowds. At the same time Sunday afternoon meetings during the fall and winter seasons were held in the Walker and Dominion theatres and other large places, and these were attended by thousands of people. During the war I addressed once a thousand Canadian soldiers in a theatre and there was great blessing.

Elim Chapel is in a flourishing condition. The work was, and is not now denominationally affiliated. There is a board of directors. Nobody is asked to join, for there is no membership roll. It is a real Christian fellowship of all who love the Lord Jesus Christ and the Truth of God.

FROM COAST TO COAST

The financial support is by free-will offerings. Finally Elim Chapel, in which frequently 750 people were crowded together in one service, became too small, and Mr. Smith purchased for the work St. Stephens Presbyterian Church on Portage Avenue, one of the principal Avenues of that growing city. This Church had for its pastor for many years Dr. Charles W. Gordon, known by the name of Ralph Connor. During the summer of 1928 it was renovated, and in October the place was dedicated as the new home of the Elim Chapel Fellowship. The seating capacity is 1500, and the auditorium is frequently filled. The services held now are as follows: Lord's day morning at ten, a meeting to remember the Lord. At eleven a regular preaching service. At three a large Sunday school of over 500 children meets. The teachers are all well-trained men and women whose aim is to lead the young to Christ. Several other Sunday schools and missions are now maintained by Elim Chapel in different parts of the City. There are "Lantern-meetings" every week in the different parts of the city.

On Sunday night there is held a large Gospel meeting. The Lord's blessing has rested upon this great service in the salvation of many. Then there is a splendid young people's society, prayer meeting and weekly Bible Study. A number of the young people of Elim Chapel dedicated their lives to work on the foreign field, and they are now at work in different foreign countries. Elim Chapel has no pastor. Mr. John Bellingham, one of the brethren who early became identified with this work, is superintendent and with the board of directors has the oversight. Each month a well-known preacher, or teacher, comes to take up the ministry of the Word. Each stays the entire month to conduct the services and to hold a week of special meetings. We mention the following who frequently visited Winnipeg: W. B. Riley, George Guille, Lewis S. Chafer, B. B. Sutcliffe, James M. Gray, Wm. Evans, A. B. Winchester, Henry Ostrom, and others. I still visit Winnipeg every year for a month's ministry. The work of Elim Chapel is far-reaching. It extends over the entire Canadian Northwest as well as into Minnesota and North Dakota, for many meetings are held every year in these border States under the leadership of Mr. Smith and Mr. Peter McFarlane of St. Paul.

How wonderful are the Lord's providential leadings! Over twenty-five years ago in carrying out my new commission I prayed for an open door in Manitoba, without knowing anybody there, except the brother from Toronto. The Lord opened the door at the right time, when young Sidney T. Smith needed help. The Lord spoke to his heart, and since then step by step, year after year I can trace His gracious leading. But how little of all this we know at the present time! What revelations we shall all have in that coming day when we shall know as we are known! Then all His servants will cry out, "What God has wrought"! What my poor sinful lips so often say down here—"Not unto me but unto Thee be the glory"—shall be the song of praise in the day of His and our glory.

Besides Winnipeg I visited other places in Manitoba. In Southern Manitoba I ministered in the German language among the Russian Mennonites in *Winkler* and *Plum Coulee*. I held a good week's meetings in *Neepawa* and also in *Brandon*. Going Westward I visited *Saskatchewan* and held services in *Regina* and in a small town, *Govan*. *Calgary* in *Alberta* was visited, but the frequent invitations from *Edmonton* I have not yet been able to accept. In *British Columbia* I visited a number of times *Vancouver* and *Victoria*, where I held conferences in different churches.

Nearly all the places in which I have ministered throughout the United States and in Canada have sent me cordial invitations for a second visit and many for a third, fourth and fifth visit. This of course is a physical impossibility. As I write out this brief sketch of my busy life, I marvel at His great goodness in keeping me as He has done, and making such a work possible. Each year gave additional proof that the step I had taken in 1899 in severing my denominational affiliation and setting out in a ministry of independence from man and dependence on Himself, had been taken under His guidance. And He will continue to guide till the work is done.

During 1925 a great agitation was started in Canada for church union. The Presbyterian, Methodist, and Congregational denominations were to form the United Church of Canada. I warned God's children wherever I could to keep away from this movement. The pastor of a certain Presbyterian church asked me to preach on the question. I did so, showing what true Christian Unity is and warning against union with modern religious infidels. When I left the church building, one of the elders was very angry and said, "The audacity of one of these Americans to come over here and tell us what to do". Well, it was done. In connection with this I must mention the parable I wrote warning against church union. I published it in *Our Hope*, and it created much amusement through all Canada.

Nine eggs had a great desire to be mixed with five other eggs. They were anxious to become 'scrambled eggs.' The nine eggs were beautiful to look upon. Their shells were white as snow. Not a speck of dirt was to be seen. Somebody had polished them as white as they could be. Nor was one of them broken or cracked. But while the outside was so beautiful their inside was a mass of corruption. The five other eggs were also nice as far as their outward appearance, nor did they have the inward corruption. Somehow the five good eggs felt that the other nine were not up to the mark. They suspected that they were bad, but perhaps not as bad as other bad eggs are. And inasmuch as the nine eggs persisted in getting in closer bonds with the five eggs, the latter finally consented to be scrambled. When the scrambling process took place the five good eggs soon discovered that they had landed in an intolerable mixture. They found out that the hope to overcome the bad odors of the nine eggs was a delusion, for the nine bad eggs overcame and spoiled completely the five good eggs. They were shocked in finding out the scrambling mistake they had made. They wept and tried hard to become unscrambled, but, lo and behold! their shells were hopelessly broken and they were unable to get themselves together again.

After a while the master of the house came and looked upon the whole mess. The scrambled eggs were very obnoxious to him and they were neither hot nor cold. And so he said, 'I will spue thee out of my mouth' (Rev. iii:16). And so the scrambled eggs perished miserably.

CHAPTER XV

WHAT a delightful thing is true Christian fellowship! To meet the members of the family of God in increasing numbers year after year brought me great blessing and also great privileges. From the very beginning of this special ministry the prayer of intercession became most precious to me. Many of those who stood by me in 1899, being fellow-helpers in prayer, are now at home with the Lord. As I went forward in this ministry I felt an increasing need of prayer, and hundreds of issues of *Our Hope* contained my deeply felt request for prayer. I sometimes feel that after all not my prayers made this ministry possible, but the hundreds who prayed for me have had a larger share in it than they realize. At the same time I have cultivated for years the ministry of intercession. I have found it very helpful to note the many prayer requests in a little book, and to carry it with me. In traveling, or sometimes in a sleepless night, the little book is opened, and then prayers ascend to the throne of grace for those whose names are before me. This is still my practice, and I have had many and most interesting experiences in this prayer life. Sometimes certain persons were especially put on my heart. The manner in which the Lord answered prayers for others was, and still is, a great encouragement to me. I also visited in scores of places the sick and the "shut ins" to pray with them. Prayers for the sick have always been a great privilege to me, and many times the Lord answered. But some experiences are sacred to me and I would rather not speak of them. If only those who are loyal to the faith could realize more the great value of intercessory prayer, and what the Lord will do through it, what miracles of His gracious power we might have!

Way down in *Texas*, on the gulf coast, on Galveston Island, a Christian was praying that the Lord might send me to that city. *Galveston* in 1900 passed through one of the greatest disasters of our country. A hurricane and tidal wave swept over it and over eight thousand lives perished. Galveston before the flood, I was told, had the reputation of being one of the hardest cities in the country. It is said that, when Mr. D. L. Moody visited Galveston, he was almost disheartened. Galveston after the flood was even worse. Yet there were a few who met in Bible Study. The leader was Judson B. Palmer, the Secretary of the Y. M. C. A., still living and, I am sure, the most beloved citizen of Galveston. He was one of the earliest subscribers to *Our Hope*, and more than once he wrote that he was praying the Lord to send me to their city to hold a Bible Conference.

In 1907 his prayers were answered, and I made my first trip to this city. The meetings were held under the auspices of the First Presbyterian and First Baptist churches and the attendance was far better than Mr. Palmer expected. I preached the Gospel on the first Sunday evening, and spoke of professing Christians, who think they are doing something in Christian service, such as singing in a choir, and who are totally ignorant of true salvation, knowing nothing of real peace. When the service was concluded a fine young lady who was in the choir turned to me with tears in her eyes and said, "I am one of those you mentioned." She accepted Christ that night.

During the week several hundred Christians came from Houston. Mr. Mordecai F. Ham, one of the outstanding Evangelists of the South, had a campaign in Houston and they came on a special train to attend the service on an afternoon. I then met my good friend Evangelist Ham for the first time. My ministry then, and my written ministry especially has been a great blessing to him, and in his great work he has scattered hundreds of my books among new converts. During my first visit to Galveston, I was entertained in the home of Mr. and Mrs. C. F. W. Felt. Mr. Felt was an engineer of the Santa Fe Railroad and a number of years later became the Chief Engineer of the entire system. He is now at home with the Lord. Several times I travelled with him in his private car and we had delightful fellowship in the things of the Lord.

Mr. Palmer was greatly encouraged in the conference we held. He had lost his family in the hurricane, but the Lord had carried him through it all. The Bible classes he had started and which he has held for some twenty-five years or more, apart from his Bible class work in the Y. M. C. A., have been greatly owned of the Lord. Some of the leading business men of Galveston thank Palmer for the shaping of their Christian characters. I saw him this year (1930) feeble in body, but still eager to hold at least one class during the week.

It was decided that I must make yearly visits to Galveston. The pastor of the First Presbyterian Church South, Dr. Robert M. Hall, had become deeply interested and we became good friends at once. For some ten years I visited Galveston every year, and nearly all the conferences were held in the First Presbyterian Church, except one year, when we met in the First Methodist Church, and during another year, when we had the services in the Y. M. C. A. in Rosenberg Hall. Through these regular visits the circle of believers and those who love His appearing increased, and many hearts were reached. One year when I spoke on Daniel and Revelation, the "Galveston News" gave daily reports of my addresses. The coloured people read them and they became quite excited when they read of the beasts and the antichrist. A number of preachers requested Mr. Palmer that some of them might be permitted to occupy the uppermost gallery in Rosenberg Hall to hear of "them beasts." The permission was given and the gallery was packed. Every once in a while, when I mentioned what would happen under antichrist, some old coloured man would say in a deep bass voice, "Good Lawd! Oh, Lawd!"

Again I think of those who were helped, enlightened, and comforted through my ministry in the island city and now they are at home with Him— Mr. and Mrs. Adriance, Mr. and Mrs. H. B. Goodman, Dr. Trueheart, Mr. Lutrell, Mr. Charles Adams and many others.

My last visit to Galveston, the year in which I write, brought a renewed and urgent invitation for another and longer visit.

In *Houston* I held numerous conferences and spoke in the First Baptist Church, in another Baptist Church, in a Brethren Hall, and in the Houston Bible Institute. One day in walking along Main Street I met Mr. Joseph Sweeney, a Roman Catholic, and a wealthy man. He stopped me and said: "Are you the man who preached last night in the Prairie Avenue Hall?" I answered, "Yes." "Well," he said, "you preached as if you meant it and believed it. But I think for an old man like me there is little hope to be saved." I asked him if I could come with him to his office in the "Chronicles Building." We went there, and I had a lengthy talk with him about salvation. I also prayed with him, but he said, "What would the people in Houston say if Joe Sweeney would get saved?" A number of years later he was saved, and became a happy Christian.

Four visits were made to *Beaumont* and well-attended conferences held in the Y. M. C. A., the First Baptist Church and in one of the Presbyterian Churches. In East Texas I made several visits to *Kirbyville.* This is a small lumber town, and while the meetings were not very large the Lord's own were greatly helped. Mr. and Mrs. T. S. Wright have stood there alone and given a loyal testimony for the Gospel by word of mouth, the printed page, and in their lives. God will reward them.

How I came to visit the capital city of Texas, *Austin,* is most interesting and shows once more the hand of the Lord. A lady had secured from my office a number of copies of "His Riches." One day she went to the home of General Webster Flanagan, who held then the office of Collector of Internal Revenue for Texas. He read the pamphlet and received, as he told me later, a great blessing. The glory of the Gospel of Jesus Christ broke upon him and filled his heart, as he said, with great peace and joy unspeakable. And so he sat down and wrote me a letter, that I must come for at least a week to Austin as his guest. He secured the First Baptist Church, and having advertised the meetings everywhere, he invited senators, state officials, and the governor. We had large audiences. He presided over the first meeting to introduce me. Now General Flanagan a number of years before had delivered in a political convention a speech, nominating a certain candidate for the presidency. In this speech he asked a question and answered it from the political viewpoint. The question was, "What are we here for?" For a long time it was a household word in the entire state. In introducing me, he reminded the audience of this question and then he said: "This gentleman whom I introduce to you has been used under God to teach me a higher answer to my question of old—'What are we here for?'" And then he said with tears in his eyes, "To live for Him who died for me."

General Flanagan was a remarkable character. In his youth he was a friend of Sam Houston. He held the office of Lieutenant Governor and other high offices. He was a great hunter. When we met, he was well up in the seventies, and he tried to persuade me to go on a hunting trip in the wild Southwestern part of the state. He passed on at over ninety years of age. I also delivered several lectures before the students of the Austin Seminary and spoke in the State University.

In *Cameron* the Baptist and Methodist churches united. I met for the first time Dr. William Dean

White a Southern Methodist preacher, and held a few years later a week's meetings with him in *Jacksonville*, Texas. Bible conferences were also held by me in *Palestine* and *Texarkana* and in *Waxahachie*.

In Waxahachie on Sunday evening, as I always do, I preached the Gospel in the Central Presbyterian Church. It was a simple discourse on "The way into the Kingdom" based on the third chapter of the Gospel of John. When I was through a young lady, a school teacher, greeted me with a happy face, telling me that while I was preaching she accepted the Lord Jesus Christ and received peace and assurance in doing so. Then she told me that she had come to this city three weeks before with a burdened heart, longing to know about the way of salvation and how to have peace. On the first Sunday she visited a church, and the preacher instead of preaching the Gospel, delivered a political harangue on making Texas dry. The next Sunday, she said, "I went to the . . . Church and the preacher read something from Browning, and made a few remarks. Oh, how I hungered to hear the Truth! Tonight my hunger is satisfied. I am saved," she said.

A Y. M. C. A. Secretary, Mr. Hunter, was instrumental in having me come to *Waco*, the seat of Baylor University. President Brookes attended some of the services, and invited me to address the students at the chapel service. I also preached in several other churches and a year later paid a second visit to Waco.

Dallas I visited for the first time when Dr. Scofield was still the pastor of the church which is now called the Scofield Memorial Church. He himself was absent. The night meetings were well attended. In the afternoons I taught a small company of excellent believers on the Epistle to the Colossians. One afternoon two strangers came to the service. They visited me the next day and made me pass an examination. They belonged to the exclusive party of the Open Brethren. I seemed to satisfy them on my conversion, though I was unable to give them the exact hour and minute, when I felt that I was born again. The next day I received a letter of rebuke signed by both of these men in which they accused me of unfaithfulness. They said they had heard me on the third chapter of Colossians and I had not mentioned "hell-fire" once, and therefore I was not a faithful witness at all and they doubted if I had any fitness for ministry whatever. Poor brethren! How I pitied them! For months after I prayed for them. In another town I sat towards evening before an open window and I heard a loud voice several blocks away, but the only words I could catch occasionally were the words "hell" and "fire". One of these men was preaching what he thought was the Gospel. But the Gospel is "good news" and not "hell-fire." Once I met one of these well-meaning men on a trip, and after talking with him, I asked him, "Where do you belong?" His answer was, "I belong to the exclusive Brethren; and where do you belong?" I replied, "I belong to the inclusive brethren." Then he wanted to know who they were, and I informed him that I include in my love and fellowship all the saints of God irrespective of name, or sect, or party; that all whom the Lord had received, I receive.

In 1924 the Evangelical Theological College was started in Dallas, and my friend Lewis S. Chafer asked me to have a part in the formation and establishment of this theological institution. Since then I have given Dallas a month every year, giving expository lectures to the coming preachers. At the same time I have held conferences in the Scofield Memorial Church and in the First Presbyterian Church, Dr. William Anderson, pastor. My time spent in Dallas in connection with the college has been a good investment and will bear fruit in the lives and ministry of the students, who have been greatly helped by my teaching.

During the war I visited *Fort Worth* three times. One conference was held in the St. Paul Methodist Church, and the other two in the First Baptist Church. Dr. R. A. Torrey was the other speaker in one of these conferences. During my yearly visits to Dallas I also visited once a week Fort Worth to speak to good audiences in the First Congregational Church.

Other places where I ministered in Texas are *Gainesville, Ballinger, Gonzales, Marshall,* and *El Paso.* El Paso I visited twice, holding conferences in the Y. M. C. A., a Methodist Church, and the Central Baptist Church. I spoke to a large Mexican audience through an interpreter during one of these visits.

Texas is a great state, I love its people and have often told them that if I had another life, I would spend it in their state.

Oklahoma was visited a number of times. *Enid* had two conferences in the Presbyterian church. North of Enid is the small Mennonite community, *Meno,* where I spent a week ministering the Word in German. I held well-attended conferences in the First Baptist church of *Oklahoma City,* of which M. F. Ham had become the pastor. One of the attendants, Mrs. Wray Loftin, was from a small town south of the capital of Oklahoma, *Paul's Valley.* She wanted to know if I would come to so small a place, not knowing that visiting small communities was a special aim in my ministry. A conference was planned in which the different churches united. The conference was held in the Presbyterian Church. And there I met Mr. and Mrs. Frank O. Ringer, who, unknown to me, had attended my meetings in Los Angeles and were readers of *Our Hope.* A second conference was held in the Methodist church, and a third one will be held, God willing, in the Presbyterian

194

Church. The Lord brought a blessing to this town not only through the oral ministry but through my books. Mr. Ringer and Mrs. Loftin were instrumental in the circulation of many books and pamphlets.

Calls also came from a number of other towns in Oklahoma. But as there seemed to be no providential leading, and the way was not opened, I did not go to these places. The Lord will send some other servant to feed His hungry sheep.

CHAPTER XVI

"I KNOW thy works; behold, I have set before thee an open door, and no man can shut it; for thou hast a little strength, and has kept my word, and hast not denied my name." (Rev. iii:8) These beautiful words came from the lips of our glorified Lord, and were addressed to the church in Philadelphia. Prophetically, Philadelphia stands for that portion of the professing church during the end days of our age which remains faithful; it is the believing remnant. The modernistic portion of the professing church is represented by Laodicea. The leading characteristics of the true remnant are given by our Lord. They keep His Word, holding it fast and obeying it, and they do not deny His Name, but exalt Him. The written Word, the Bible, and the living Word, our Lord Jesus Christ, are attacked and rejected in professing Christendom. Behind it all stands the enemy of all truth, who, when he spoke for the first time in human history, injected doubt as to God having spoken (Genesis iii:i). And when that being spoke the first time in the New Testament, he raised the question—"If Thou be the Son of God?" (Matthew iv:3). The inspiration and revelation of the Bible and the Deity of Jesus Christ our Lord—this is the battlefield of these last days.

196

And the Lord speaks of His faithful ones, "Thou hast a little strength." I once visited a sick brother who had been very ill. They told me that he was better and had a little strength again. But when I saw him, he was a picture of perfect weakness. The little strength means acknowledged weakness. This little strength leads the true believer to cast himself on the Lord for strength and everything else. And here is His gracious assurance, "I have set before thee an open door, and no man can shut it."

These words have been very precious to me from the very start of my new commission. To be true to Him and to His Word has been my constant aim, as well as to maintain that little strength, which makes one dependent on Him. He has not failed His promise of the open door. How wonderfully He has led forward and opened doors for ministry, and heart doors as well!

In 1895 I met a godly brother from New Jersey, Mr. David Wilson Moore. He needed special spiritual help which I was able to give him through the grace of God. I visited him in Clayton, N. J., and a number of years later he retired from business and moved to Colorado Springs. In 1904 he invited me to come to *Colorado Springs* and to hold a conference there in the First Presbyterian Church. This started my ministry in that delightful city. I visited *Colorado* for ten years, mostly during the summer, and held each year a Bible Conference in the First Presbyterian Church, in the First Congregational Church, in the First Christian Church, and in the Y. M. C. A. The majority of conferences were held in the First Presbyterian Church. Many tourists from all sections of the country attended these services and received a blessing. "I heard you in Colorado Springs"—"I attended your meetings in Colorado"—"I was in your conference in Colorado Springs." I have heard this perhaps a hundred times in different parts of the country.

And how I enjoyed the beautiful surroundings! As much as my time allowed I climbed among the mountains, watched wild life, and enjoyed God's great out-doors.

Twice I held conferences in the Congregational Church of *Manitou*.

In *Pueblo* and *Trinidad* I held also successful conferences, but my larger work was done in *Denver*. After my meetings at the Springs I went to Denver on the invitation of Mr. Taussig, a Hebrew Christian believer, and Mr. Sadler. The meetings were held in a small Congregational church. I made yearly visits to Denver after that and urged the interested preachers to form the Rocky Mountain Bible Conference Association, which was done; these conferences still continue. They were held for a number of years in the Twenty-Third Avenue Presbyterian Church, P. V. Jenness, pastor. Three conferences were held by me in

Boulder. A certain modernistic preacher made great objections to my coming, and went so far as to warn his people (but not the Lord's people) to stay away from my services. He said that I was not a fit teacher to listen to in these days of progress and advanced thought. As it was reported to me, he said, "This gentleman believes in the exploded theory of the verbal inspiration of the Bible. He also teaches the theory of substitution, but the worst is, he teaches that foolish idea that Jesus is actually coming again from heaven. He gave me a fine advertisement for the people came to hear this "old fogey" (the title conferred upon me by some modernists), and received a rich blessing.

In the adjoining state *Kansas* I ministered in *Kansas City* and in *Pittsburgh.* In *Pretty Prairie,* in a large German Mennonite Community, I addressed for a week their General Conference which was attended by a large number of preachers and delegates. I also visited other Mennonite communities in Kansas, speaking to them in the German language.

Two brethren at work among the Indians, Mr. Butler and Mr. Frey, requested me to come to *Flagstaff, Arizona.* They had it upon their hearts to start a Southwestern Bible Conference which missionaries at work among the Navajo and Hopi Indians and their converts might attend. In 1911 I held my first conference there in the Presbyterian Church. I met a number of the brethren at work on the Indian reservations, and several Christian Indians attended. Mrs. Gertrude Lewis Gates, who took a great interest in the work among the different tribes, was also present. The next year led me again to Flagstaff and the Conference was held in the Methodist Church. Under the leadership of F. G. Mitchell and others a large tract of land was secured from the United States government to locate a summer camp at *Cliffs*, at the foot of Eldin Mountain, not far from the majestic San Francisco Peaks, towering thirteen thousand feet above sea level. Nearby lumber mills supplied lumber to erect a few shacks and a large building for meetings and a dining hall. Next year the conference met in the new place, and the Southwestern Bible Conference Association was organized. I attended several more of these conferences, and each time I pass the camp on the Santa Fe, on my way to California, I remember the pleasant and blessed times I had with the brethren in the beginning of this movement.

Northern Arizona is beautiful. Because of the altitude of seven thousand feet, while the summer days are hot, the nights are cool. The air is charged with the exhalations of the great pines and the fragrant wild flowers. The whole region is of volcanic origin, and lava beds are found everywhere. Being such a lover of nature, I

IN ARIZONA. MR. GAEBELEIN IS AT THE RIGHT

climbed round the rocks and admired the flora
so abundant everywhere.

Through a friend I was enabled to spend a
whole week at the Grand Canyon of the Colorado River in Arizona. How I enjoyed the
gorgeous scenery! Daily I made trips down the
trails to study the interesting story of geology
as revealed by this wonder of nature. The
Indians say that when the gods produced the
great canyon, in places more than six thousand
feet deep, they took the earth and stones they
dug up, and put it all in two heaps, and thus the
two peaks of the San Francisco range were created. Both peaks are gloriously seen from Flagstaff and from the Canyon. The Indian conception is not half so bad as some of the speculations
of cultured and learned evolutionists. The work
among the Indians has brought gracious results
and some have been saved from the lowest forms
of idolatry. I had several invitations to attend a
snake dance, with its vile ceremonies, followed by
certain obscene practises and orgies. I refused and
told the friends who urged me to go and see, that
I could not conscientiously watch these poor
heathen dancing around and thus encourage them
in their degrading idolatry.

In 1911 I also visited *Phoenix*, having received
the invitation from the Y. M. C. A. secretary.
I did not know a person in Phoenix and feared
we might not have many people coming to the

meetings, for it was, I believe, the first attempt to hold a conference there. One day, while making nature studies back of Flagstaff, I met a gentleman. In talking with him I found that he was Dr. Atwood, Protestant Episcopal Bishop of Arizona, whose residence is in Phoenix. I told him of my coming visit, and he knew of it and encouraged the services by his presence. They were held in the Southern Methodist church. It was a strange sight to see ushers in shirt sleeves on Sunday morning. I soon wished that I might be permitted to preach in shirt sleeves too, for it was around 102. I wore my heavy northern Prince Albert coat and a vest besides. But the heat is dry and one does not perspire as much as in the East. The services were well attended and were climaxed on Sunday afternoon by a great out-door meeting on the Plaza. It was an interesting sight to see hundreds of people sitting round in the grass and under palm trees. There were many Mexicans, women and girls gaudily dressed, a number of Indians and half breeds. In simple language I gave them the story of the Christ who died for all. And such attention! I am sure I shall find some in glory who accepted the Gospel call in that service.

Each time I passed through *Albuquerque, New Mexico*, and that was at least sixteen times, a beloved brother, now with the Lord, W. E. Mauger, came to the station for a chat and through him

I was privileged to hold two Bible Conferences in this city. One of these was held in the Presbyterian church, all other Protestant churches uniting. The pastor did not promise great things and feared that apart from Lord's day the meetings would be insignificantly small. There was a fine audience in the morning and much to the surprise of the pastor a larger audience gathered at night. His prophecy of small meetings did not come true. The audiences increased and filled the large auditorium every night. On Wednesday night one of the pastors arose after my address. He said that he had made a discovery through these services. He and the other preachers had complained about the meagre attendance in the different churches and had used different means to interest the people. Then he said, "Here comes a man preaching nothing but the Word of God in a simple, instructive, and constructive way, and the crowds have increased. I think our people want to have the Bible preached and I shall do so in the future." The whole audience broke out in prolonged applause.

CHAPTER XVII

M Y FIRST book was published in 1900, and since then almost two score of books and numerous pamphlets have been written and published by me. Many times have I been asked why I did not have my books published by one of the larger publishing houses. Only my *Harmony of the Prophetic Word* is published by the Fleming H. Revell Company and *The Christ we Know* by the Bible Institute Colportage Association.

There are two reasons why I have acted as my own publisher. Large firms have big overhead expenses and they have to demand higher prices, especially for books which are not big sellers. My volumes on Daniel and Revelation have each 240 pages. A leading New York publisher expressed several years ago a desire to take over these two books, advertise them well, and make them both good sellers. But he asked me to make the price one dollar and fifty cents. I sell them at eighty-five cents postpaid, and much less when they are taken in larger quantities for Bible classes. I published my own works so that they might be sold, without much commercial gain, at the lowest possible price, so as to make them available for all. I suppose that this is one of the reasons why some of my books have passed through fifteen and more editions.

And there is another reason. Thousands of the Lord's people are poor; they cannot afford to buy many books. There are also country preachers with small salaries, foreign missionaries and other Christian workers who need suitable literature. "Freely ye have received, freely give" has always been practised by me, and for many years I have given away thousands of books and pamphlets. If another publisher had published my works this would have been financially impossible, for I would have had to pay for each copy. Hundreds of libraries have received copies of my books free. Many colleges, seminaries, and other institutions of learning have them on their shelves. Many a young preacher starting in life has been supplied with them and they have been a great blessing to many. They have gone to the foreign missionaries to cheer their hearts and not a few have translated portions into native tongues. I still do this work under His gracious blessing and shall continue to do so. Many of my friends have assisted in this phase of ministry. We shall find in His presence a blessed harvest.

And so I have done with *Our Hope*. Whenever someone writes of being too poor to pay the subscription any longer, or being sick and having no income, my office has the instruction to put them on the free list.

It was in the beginning of 1900 that I received a letter from a Texas farmer whose harvest had failed and he wrote to have his subscription discontinued. I wrote him a nice letter and told him he would receive it free. In addition I sent him several pamphlets and a copy of my *Studies in Zechariah*. I was not a little surprised when this brother wrote me three years later, in 1903, from Los Angeles, sending an invitation to come as his guest to California and hold a series of meetings in this city. When I accepted the call, he wired the money for the expenses and something over. They had discovered oil on his farm; he had sold out and had become well-to-do and then moved to Los Angeles. I had often prayed that the Lord might open a door for ministry on the Pacific coast and here was His answer.

For the first time I travelled on the Santa Fe railroad. The first trip convinced me there could not be a better way to reach Southern California than by this great system. The scenery is wonderful, passing through Raton and the Glorietta passes, and even greater after leaving Ashfork. The Harvey eating houses furnish the best meals of any railroad system in the United States and Canada. The same system furnishes equally good accommodations to Oklahoma and Texas.

I went to *Los Angeles* in the early fall of 1903. Mr. Ralph D. Smith, the head of the Los Angeles Bible House, made the necessary arrangements. A hall was rented and some advertising done. I had but a few readers in Los Angeles, but the attendance was good and the ministry greatly blessed by the Lord. There were some definite cases of blessing and His seal rested upon the work done. Mr. Smith brought with him a gentleman, whom I then met for the first time, Mr. Lyman Stewart, later the President of the Union Oil Company. He attended every service and was deeply interested. His interest was so great that when I went from Southern California to San Francisco, he followed me there to attend the meetings. He received then the first impulse to establish a big Bible Institute in Los Angeles. Later Mr. T. C. Horton and Dr. A. C. Dixon came to that city, and Mr. Lyman Stewart carried out his plans, and as a result that magnificent institution known as the Los Angeles Bible Institute is in existence.

I did not return to Los Angeles until Dr. Reuben A. Torrey was the Dean of the Institute. But from 1915 on, I made eight visits to this great city on the Pacific Coast. The Bible Institute in 1915 was in process of construction and Dr. Torrey had arranged for my conference in the Immanuel Presbyterian church. The conference was very successful. On Sunday afternoon I addressed an audience of 4,000 people in the Temple Auditorium on "Modern Day Delusions." They needed such a lecture on the coast, and now fifteen years later they need it still more, for every cult under the sun is flourishing in Los Angeles.

When the Institute was completed, Mr. Lyman Stewart asked me to come and inaugurate a summer Bible Conference work. Dr. Torrey thought it could not be done, for people rush to the sea-shore and to the mountains. I accepted the invitation and in 1916 began this summer work on the coast. I preached three times each Lord's day and had a regular course of Bible instruction covering several weeks during the month of August. The audiences increased, and on the last Sunday on my first visit I had 1,500 in each service on Lord's day. In 1918 I find this entry in my journal: "What a wonderful opportunity! Yesterday was one of the greatest days in this God-given ministry. I preached in the morning to over 2,500 people. The afternoon meeting was even larger and the evening service as large as the morning service. Mr. Stewart seemed to be very happy." My meetings for Bible instruction filled the lower auditorium night after night. That there was great blessing needs not to be stated. Letters upon letters were received by me from those who were led into the light through my testimony both in Gospel preaching and teaching. I also found the results scattered all over this continent, for many tourists from different states were in the audiences. On one of my last visits, I think it was in 1922, a lady stepped to the front to greet me. She expressed herself enthusiastically over what she had heard. She said how very much it had helped her and opened her eyes to many things. She wanted *Our Hope* and later ordered my books for study. She handed me her card and it informed me the lady was Miss Christobel Pankhurst, living then in Hollywood. Since that time Miss Pankhurst has become an interesting lecturer and writer on prophetic truths.

In 1919 Mr. Lyman Stewart suggested that I move to the coast. He and his brother Mr. Milton Stewart thought that I should become the Editor of a much larger religious magazine. Mr. Lyman Stewart offered to put up the necessary funds and finance this undertaking. He even suggested the name to be *Our Hope and Our Work*; that is, a combination of *Our Hope* and *The King's Business*. It did not take me long to make my decision. *Our Hope* has a distinctive testimony to bear. The Lord Himself had entrusted me with it, and after prayer the Lord gave grace and courage to decline the magnificent offer.

I was happy in 1929 to greet, in another visit to the Institute, so many old friends, but the Stewarts are no longer here but have joined the waiting saints above.

My California ministry was not confined to Los Angeles, but I covered many other places in the state. My first visit to *San Diego* took place in 1903 when I addressed German and English meetings. Four times more I was permitted to minister in this city. One incident I cannot pass by. In some way the First Church of the Nazarene had been opened for a two weeks ministry. One evening when I was speaking on "Christ the Wisdom and Power of God," just as I was about beginning to preach, I noticed that quite a company of men and women came and took the remaining back seats. They left immediately after the sermon.

Then one of my hearers came up and said: "Do you know that you had Mrs. Aimee Semple McPherson and her party in your audience tonight? They were so sorry not to meet you personally, but they had to rush to make the last car. But she gave me a message for you." I am sorry, but my pen refuses to write down the polished words of flattery and sweet compliments my ear had to hear. Then this man said, "I know her well and shall see her next week. Have you a message for her?" I replied "Yes. Tell her she can catch flies with honey, but not A. C. G." I never heard from her again.

I note in passing a few other places where I spoke, in some for several seasons—*Santa Paula, Santa Barbara, Riverside, Redlands, Escondido, Hemet, Long Beach, Redondo Beach, Santa Monica, San Jose, Balboa, Whittier, Pasadena, Oakland,* and *San Francisco.* San Francisco I visited twice in 1903, holding my first conference in a Brethren Hall. Then I had an urgent call to come again in

beginning of April in 1906. I was anxious to go
and prayed about it. After prayer I was undecided.
I wanted to visit the brethren again, but something
seemed to say that I should not go. As this
impression became stronger I declined, and accepted a call from Dayton, Ohio. How I praised
the Lord, when one morning during the week I
might have been in San Francisco, I saw the
startling headlines "San Francisco destroyed by
an earthquake and fire." A few years later I
held successful meetings in the Hamilton Square
Baptist Church. They told me my meetings were
the best attended evangelical services for a
number of years. In leaving my hotel I noticed
one day a big church building, the First Congregational Church. Dr. Aked, the well known
modernist, was the pastor. His topic for an
address announced on the bulletin board was so
unusual that I noted it down. He was to speak
on "The Meditation of a Jackass." I shall tell
my readers later what good use I made of it when
it was needed.

To show how the Lord opened doors I mention
the different denominations among which I
worked on the coast: Methodist, Baptist, Presbyterian, United Presbyterian, Church of the
Disciples, Reformed, Protestant Episcopal, Nazarene, United Brethren, Church of the Brethren,
Mennonites, Plymouth Brethren, and Congregational. In all these denominations there are the

true children of God, known to the great Shepherd of the sheep, the glorified Head of His church. And He sends forth His servants to minister unto their need. I believe one of the great revelations which await us on that coming day, when we shall be gathered home, will be the knowledge of His gracious providences. We know but little now how He guided in His service, but what will it be when all the hidden things will be brought to light!

Much literature was freely circulated in all places in California where I ministered, and during the great exhibitions in San Diego and San Francisco many thousands of copies of *His Riches* and warnings against delusive cults were handed to the visitors. I sent 10,000 copies of *His Riches*, 5,000 copies of *Joseph and His Brethren*, thousands of other pamphlets and tracts, thousands of Bible Study pamphlets and *Rightly Dividing the Word of Truth* with thousands of copies of *Our Hope* to San Francisco. Mr. George W. Hunter, who had charge of this work, sent the following communication:

"Just this word from me to let you know how things are going at the Exposition; I am having the greatest experience I have ever had every day. The hungry hearts that I am having the privilege of feeding are many each day.

"The booklet *His Riches* is going well and those who receive them seem very glad to get them and many speak of having a great desire to read it. Some have read it and come back for more to send to friends, others have taken it, read it and returned to thank me for giving it to them. The copies of *Our Hope* are also being received by the many who are glad to take them and read them. I am not crowding them on any one, and the wisdom of that is manifest, as not one booklet or tract that I have given away has been dropped on the floor.

"I am almost out of *Joseph and His Brethren*. I have been judicious in the distribution, as I did not want to have one copy lose its mark, and so I have been trying to distribute them wherever I can to Jews. I have had a number of talks with Jews, and I am satisfied that the Lord has been pleased with the fruit of these conferences. I shall need more of them by the time you can get this and order some for me.

"If you have anything else that will magnify the Messiah for Jews I shall be glad if you care to add it to the list, as the opportunity to sow seed is the mightiest I have ever had, and I feel sure if you could step in and see it for yourself you would heartily coincide with me.

"The eagerness with which the people receive the Bible Study literature is inspiring indeed. One minister said: 'I am mighty glad to get this very suggestive evidence; I shall use every bit of it in my work and you will hear from me later.' One to-day from Pennsylvania said: 'This is splendid. I am mighty glad to receive it.' Another from Japan said: 'I am taking all this home and you can rest assured that it will not be put away but used over and over again.' Another, a young man from Maryland, said when I showed him the several pieces of Bible Study: 'Can I have this? and can I have another set for my brother who is a minister? I know he is just eager to get just this kind of Bible Study and I shall be mighty glad to be able to carry it home to him.' Within five minutes after he left, a young high-school teacher from Oklahoma who is also a member of the Y. W. C. A. said, 'I have a class of young women at home and this kind of Bible Study is just what I have been seeking. Can I get more when I get home?'

"This will show the eagerness with which the Bible Study is being received. Any more that you may have I can use with great profit, as I have never seen such an opportunity for this kind of work."

It was a great testimony and I shall expect a rich harvest in that day.

CHAPTER XVIII

NEXT to the spiritual blessings the gift for which I have thanked the Lord most has been the good constitution and good health which I have enjoyed all my life, and without which the work I have been privileged in doing would have been impossible. But while I firmly believe in the protecting care of the heavenly Father and in the power of the Lord whom I serve, I also believe in taking care of myself and in the use of proper food and all other means to preserve health and strength. Gluttony is as much a sin as drunkenness; over-eating has disastrous results. The intemperate use of coffee and tea, which I have noticed in some Bible teachers, undermines the nervous system and influences the heart action.

Some Christians think that a preacher or Bible teacher should make a martyr of himself by denying himself the better accommodations. There used to be a good brother in Kansas City who practised a morbid economy. He would not take a Pullman to save a little money for missionary purposes, and as for taking proper food, he almost starved himself at certain times. The result was that he undermined his constitution and was sickly. It reminds me of Charles H. Spurgeon. At a time when he was nervously exhausted he went on a trip and bought for himself a whole compartment on a railroad train. A certain friend heard of it and rebuked the great preacher, asking him, "Are you not afraid to waste the Lord's money?" He answered quickly, "Brother, what about the Lord's body?"

I came once to a certain city and the man who had made the arrangements took me to a lodging house, where beds could be gotten for twenty-five cents for the night. I asked him if there was a better place in town and he answered there was, but it would cost at least two dollars a day to have a room there and the eating was expensive. I told the brother to take me there, and if necessary I would pay my own bill. In another place a small, dark, hall room with no means of ventilation was to be my home for ten days, and, as better accommodations were possible, I went there. In still another town, to save money I was expected to eat in a lunch wagon. They took me there with the assurance that it was one of the best places in town. The waiter took with his dirty hands a piece of butter, and put it on my plate, and the flies were contaminating everything. I said, "You can save money but not on me; I cannot do the Lord's work under such conditions." But these are but a few of many similar cases.

I suppose somebody talked about these occurrences, and then the report was circulated that I refused to go places where no good hotel accommo-

dations were available.   But that is not the truth.
In scores of small towns and villages where I
ministered I was perfectly satisfied with conditions, and I never refused an invitation, or call,
to a place because it lacked hotel accommodations.
But in places where better comforts were available
I felt that the Lord's servant is entitled to them.
Much self-denial is connected with such a ministry.

Since 1899, when I accepted this ministry, I
have been enabled through His grace not to turn
aside from it.   Loved ones are still living in the
Fatherland, brothers and sister and their families.
How they have begged for a visit for well nigh
thirty years!   More than once I decided that I
would take a trip abroad, but when the time
came, the love of the work and the love of souls
kept me here.   I felt deeply that I must be
faithful to my calling.   Twice wealthy brethren
offered me trips to Egypt and the Holy Land.   I
could not accept, for it would have meant three
months turning aside from the work.   Perhaps
some day it may become possible and if not, I
shall be happy in the work till He comes.   Furthermore I have received repeated invitations to come
to Great Britain for ministry and several calls have
come from Australia and New Zealand.   Once I
was urged to visit the mission stations in China,
and a few years ago the American representative of
the Czecho-Slovakian Republic suggested that I

visit that country in the interest of the Gospel, giving me a personal letter of introduction to President Masaryk. I could not tear myself away from the work here and had no liberty to leave the field in this country into which the Lord had called me.

I have yet to give an interesting account of the work done in the North Pacific States. I take the State of *Idaho* first. My first visit to this state was when I held a week's meetings in *Twin Falls*. A Presbyterian preacher, Mr. McGillivray, had sent the invitation. A week's meetings were held, different churches uniting. On Lord's day the meetings were held in the High School Auditorium which brought out very large congregations. I found out later that a number of people accepted Christ as their Saviour in this town.

A beloved brother, Mr. C. J. Franklin, C. E., was instrumental in holding conferences in the City of *Boise*. On a certain evening when I gave my lecture on the "Jewish Question," an exposition of the eleventh chapter in the Epistle to the Romans, a well-dressed, tall gentleman came to the service, and as he attracted attention, I felt he must be a man of note. He paid the strictest attention. When the service was over he came up and said, "My name is Moses Alexander. I am the Governor of this state, and I want to let you know how very much I enjoyed your discourse. Can you come tomorrow morning to my office at the Capitol? If I am in the Senate, tell my secretary who you are."

Now Mr. Alexander is a Hebrew and a fine
gentleman. I was glad for the opportunity.
When I met him in his office, he expressed again
his delight over my lecture, and said that it should
be given in every city of the States. He offered
to write a personal letter to the mayors of any
cities of his own state, if I should visit to give this
lecture. But then he expressed disagreement with
my views that the Jewish people are still a nation
and God's people. He thought assimilation was the
only future of the Jews. I took my little Bible
from my pocket and said, "Governor, here are
your own prophets; I am sure you believe in them.
May I read you something?" Then I read as
follows: "Thus saith the Lord, which giveth the
sun for a light by day, and the ordinances of the
moon and of the stars for a light by night, which
divideth the sea when the waves thereof roar—the
Lord of Hosts is His Name. If those ordinances
depart from before Me, saith the Lord, then the
seed of Israel also shall cease from being a nation
from before Me for ever. Thus saith the Lord, if
heaven above can be measured, and the foundations of the earth searched out beneath, I will also
cast off all the seed of Israel for all that they have
done, saith the Lord" (Jeremiah xxxi:35-37).
After reading I turned to him and said: "Well
Governor, the sun, the moon and the stars are
still shining nor has man measured heaven above
and the foundations of the earth beneath. What

have you to say?" He confessed himself defeated.

Governor Alexander also spoke to me of his past, telling about the many sufferings he had had and explaining how he was then in his second term as State Governor. He added, "And who is better fitted to govern than one who has suffered?" How true! Yes, One has suffered for our sins and He will yet be the Governor of all the nations, the King of kings and the Lord of lords.

Later in the week I dined with him in his home. Some months after he appointed me a commissioner to represent his state in a certain national convention. When I visited Boise again, he attended my meetings and seemed to receive help through them. Many other calls have come to me from Boise, Nampa and other Idaho towns, but I have not been able to visit the state again.

My first visit to the State of *Washington* was made in 1903. Mr. Osgood asked me to tarry for a week in *Tacoma*. The meetings were held in a small Baptist Church and in the Y. M. C. A. Later, when Dr. Clarence W. Weyer had become the pastor of the First Presbyterian Church, I held another Bible Conference in Tacoma. It was a very well attended conference. Great blessing rested upon the ministry. There was at that time in the Congregational Church of Tacoma a young preacher by the name of Dyer, who attempted to make his reputation by being liberal. My program, which included several addresses on the return of our Lord, had been circulated several weeks ahead of my arrival. This Congregational preacher evidently was very much opposed to that blessed hope, as all modernists and liberalists are. One day during my meetings, somebody handed me a card announcing that the Sunday after I had left Tacoma, the celebrated Dr. Charles F. Aked, pastor of the First Congregational Church of San Francisco, would give a lecture in Dyer's Church on "The Frantic Nonsense of the Second Coming of Christ."

I asked Dr. Weyer when we might expect the largest congregation during the week, and he told me, "On the prayer meeting night." On that night the church was filled to overflowing; probably nearly a thousand people were present. In the middle of my sermon I took up the card and read the announcement of the coming of Charles F. Aked to deliver a lecture in answer to my discourses on the return of Christ. Then I stopped and said: "Friends, last week I was in San Francisco. One day when I left the St. Francis Hotel I passed a church. The pastor had announced a peculiar theme on which he was to speak. It was very sensational, 'The Meditation of a Jackass.' Well, the preacher who talked on that was none other than the Dr. Charles F. Aked who is coming to speak on 'The Frantic Nonsense of Christ's Return.' So, friends, if you want to hear the meditations of a jackass just go and hear him. But remember the Lord Almighty looks on and when he sees this poor little fellow denying His Word and ridiculing the Truth of God, He looks down from heaven and says, 'The meditations of a jackass.'"

Well, it brought down the house. Dr. Weyer found out that only about thirty people listened to the famous meditations in the Congregational church. In 1929 I visited Tacoma again and we had great meetings in the beautiful new First Presbyterian Church. The audiences were phenomenally large during the entire week. Many old friends greeted me and I found the blessed after-results of my former visits. My friend Dr. Weyer seemed to be anxious to leave Tacoma. He asked me to pray about a call which had come to him from Duluth. After prayer I gave him my impression and told him to remain in Tacoma. I talked earnestly to him about it, but he seemed to think that he should accept the call. When saying good-bye to him at the station, I said again, "Brother Weyer stay here. The people want you to stay; your work is not finished." I did not know it would be the last time that I should look into his face. He went to Duluth and a few months later was suddenly called home to be with the Lord.

Seattle I have visited a number of times, holding conferences in the First Presbyterian Church, which has the largest membership of any Presbyterian Church in the world. My friend, Dr. Mark

A. Matthews, the pastor, received a great blessing through my first visit over ten years ago. He saw the great importance of the premillennial coming of our Lord and prophecy in general, and began at once to preach it. Since then I have made several visits to Seattle. The last one a year ago (1929) was very successful. The Church, which seats some 2,500, was full on Lord's day morning, and in the afternoon I had over 1,500 with another full house at night. Speaking in the afternoon on the glory and the power of the Word of God I said, "The greatest menace in this country is not the bootlegger, but the college professor who rejects the Bible and undermines the faith of the young." I also paid my compliments to the anti-christian evolution theory. I was surprised to find myself and my remarks on Monday morning on the first page of Seattle's leading newspaper *The Post Intelligence*. The reporter had not only reported me correctly, but he had gone to the professor of Zoology and Biology in the State University, who answered my charge. Somewhat of a debate followed in the same paper, and it ended with the victory on my side. This publicity was a fine advertisement for the services, and the large audiences both afternoons and evenings remained with me. The Lord gave great blessing through the ministry of His Word. *North Yakima* or, as it is now called *Yakima*, was opened through Mr. George Hunt. I have already mentioned his name in connection with Staples, Minnesota, where he had carried on a good Gospel work. When he purchased a fruit orchard in Yakima, he continued his evangelistic ministry and before long a small gathering was formed. I held two conferences with good attendance and blessing in this town. Repeated invitations to return were out of my reach. I had meetings in *Walla-Walla* and in *Vancouver, Washington*. In *Everett* and *Bellingham* I had conferences. The city of *Spokane* had three visits from me. Mr. C. R. Scafe had written me frequently from *Potlach*, Idaho, and told me how my written ministry had helped him in the knowledge of the truth. Then he became pastor of the Fourth Presbyterian church in Spokane. I had two conferences with him. The third visit was in connection with a Swedish Mission Church. Numerous other places *Wenatchee, Ellenville, Olympia* and smaller towns sent calls, but as there were no providential leadings, I did not make a visit.

One more state remains, the state of *Oregon*. The evangelistic committee of the Congregational Church in Oregon, headed by Mr. Robert Millard, invited me to come to *Portland*, and the committee made all necessary arrangements. The largest church auditorium in Portland is the White Temple, a Baptist Church. The late W. B. Hinson was the pastor. This great auditorium was secured and I held my first conference there in

1915. The church was filled to the last seats in every service. It was one of the most successful conferences I ever held. A large number of people became readers of my magazine, and I was told that as a result of this conference a number of churches had Bible study revivals.

A year later I held the second conference and this time in another section of this beautiful city. Dr. Staub, pastor of the Sunnyside Congregational Church, invited me to hold the week's services in his church auditorium. Dr. Staub is one of the few Congregationalists who is loyal to the faith and a strong believer in the return of our Lord. The conference was well attended and blessings resulted once more.

Then came my third visit. Several of the officers of the First Congregational Church had heard me, and very much to my surprise they requested that my next conference should be held in their church building. Now the First Congregational Church has the reputation of being modernistic. Their pastor was Dr. Dyott, and when the matter was brought up in the church council he objected strenuously against holding the conference in the First Congregational Church. But the interested officers voted that I should be invited and that the church building be put at my disposal.

Now Dr. Dyott was a perfect gentleman. He was frank to say that he did not agree at all with my views, but he welcomed me very graciously

and acted as a perfect Christian gentleman.
Moreover, he attended every service and was a
most attentive listener. He was pleased to see
the big church auditorium with its galleries filled
by so many people. Once more the Lord sent a
great blessing through my ministry. When I bid
Dr. Dyott adieu, I asked him if he would accept
a number of my works. He seemed to be very
much pleased, and so I sent him eight or ten of my
books. Two months later I received a very cordial
letter, thanking me for the books and saying that
he had enjoyed them. He added that he hoped
that in all my future visits to Portland his church
would be opened to my ministry. He urged me
not to consider any other invitation. What had
happened to him, a modernistic preacher? I do
not know, for in the same year he passed from this
earthly scene and I did not meet him again. But
I have the deep impression that my ministry and
my books had been used with him.

Last year (1929) I had another delightful conference in Portland, receiving the invitation
through my friend Dr. B. B. Sutcliffe, the pastor
of the Calvary Presbyterian Church. Dr. Sutcliffe, whom I met some thirty years before in
St. Joseph, Missouri, held several large Bible
classes in Portland every week. I was there on
Easter Sunday and the church was packed; in
fact people had to be turned away. So I was glad
that I could preach once more in the large White

Temple, and the same audiences greeted me there as fourteen years ago. I was told that I had attained the reputation of being the only Bible teacher who could fill the White Temple. Many of the old friends welcomed me. Several told me that my former visits had brought them to the knowledge of the Gospel. The blessings ran high once more, and hundreds requested an early return.

South of Portland is the city of *Albany*. On the invitation of the pastor of the United Presbyterian Church, Dr. W. P. White, now President of the Los Angeles Bible Institute, I held two conferences in his church. We had a blessed Christian fellowship together, and the Lord's blessing rested upon the Word I preached and taught. There seemed to have been a tendency among some of the hearers to accept the theory of faith healing. Dr. White told me of a certain preacher who had been in Albany and who had advocated divine healing. The meetings were held in a hall with waxed floors on which one of the prominent Christian ladies had slipped and in falling had broken her hip. Dr. White told the Bible teacher that here was a good chance to demonstrate the truth of divine healing, but though prayer was made, there was no answer so far as the instantaneous healing was concerned.

After Dr. White left, a certain Pentecostal delusionist and faith healer came to Albany and succeeded in dividing hopelessly the United Presbyterian Church. As if the Holy Spirit ever divided the flock of God!

I have borne for many years an unflinching testimony against all unscriptural and fanatical cults and teachings. I mean by these such cults as Christian Science; Spiritism; Russellism, known now as the International Bible Students Association; Seventh Day Adventism; Pentecostalism; McPhersonism; Faith Healing Cults, and extreme Sanctificationists. My book on the "Healing Question" has achieved much success in delivering people out of the clutches of certain pious frauds who go about under the camouflage of the highest Christian profession and using hypnotic powers (if not something worse) deceive the people and get rich on the misfortunes of others. Words fail me in condemning these women and men, who with their audacious pretensions, lead astray the sheep of Christ. What an awful judgment will fall upon them some day! But unmasking error and being outspoken on these things draws the fire of the enemy. I have been often maligned by the faith healers and their friends and have been hated by these delusionists.

Twice I have been in *Baker City* in Eastern Oregon and a conference was also held by me in *Milton*. One of my sons, about fourteen years ago, was a mining engineer in a wild region of Northeastern Oregon in *Cornucopia*. It could be reached only by a 75 mile ride in an old fashioned stage-coach. I paid him a visit and being obliged to stay over night in a small half-way mountain village, I spoke in a small church to a few people and gave them the Gospel. I met several elderly people there who had never had a ride on a railroad, in fact who had never seen a railroad train.

Sometimes I have been asked if I would like to live my life over again. Yes, I would, if I could live it for Him and in His service; and then I would go to such small places, to mountain villages, to hamlets, to minister to the poor and to the neglected. Such work is greatly needed in this country. Perhaps the Lord will commission another young man and send him with His Gospel and His Truth to these places.

CHAPTER XIX

"AND JACOB served seven years for Rachel; and they seemed unto him but a few days, for the love he had for her." (Genesis xxix:20.) I have served Him for fifty years, and I can say, "Verily these fifty years seem to me but a short time." A service rendered through constraining love is more than joy. What happy, joyful years they have been, these fifty years! How quickly they have passed, as all our lives pass quickly. "We spend our years as a tale is told." (Ps. xc:9.) "For what is your life? It is even a vapour, that appeareth for a little time, and then vanisheth away." (James iv:14.) His yoke is easy, His burden is light. If the servant of Christ serves Him, and *only Him*, walks in His fellowship, remembers the glorious Person, whom he serves, then this service is not only easy and light, but it becomes the most glorious occupation. It has been so with me. "Ye serve the Lord Christ," has echoed and re-echoed in my heart.

Now I might have said a good deal more about the imperfect service I have given Him, who alone is worthy. I might have recorded my many failures, my weaknesses, my neglects. Some Christians seemed to have reached such a high state, that they say they cannot sing any more—

"Prone to wander, Lord, I feel it." I do not belong to this class. I have a poor, wandering heart. With David I say, "Thou tellest my wanderings." And many tears have been wept in confessing humiliation. "Put Thou my tears into Thy bottle; are they not in Thy book?" (Ps. lvi:8.) Yes, He knows these tears and has recorded them all. At the close of fifty years of untiring service, with self-sacrifice, and self-denial, I realize as never before "that in my flesh there dwelleth no good thing." All the good that is in me, all the good that I possess, all the good I have done, is all of Him; it is all of grace. How patient, how kind, how loving, how forgiving He has been with me! The one great aim in all my service has been to exalt the Lord Jesus Christ. When I was a boy, the Spirit of God gave to my young mind the reality of the Lord. I had a godly teacher, a young candidate for the Lutheran ministry, and he taught the class of boys a little German verse.

> Gieb mir Deinen Frieden
> Alle Tag hinieden
> Schenk mir Deinen Heil'gen Geist,
> Der mich stets zu Jesus weist.

Translated into prose it means this: "Give me Thy peace, every day down here give me Thy Holy Spirit, who points me to Jesus." My young lips prayed that little prayer faithfully for years, though I was not conscious of the full meaning of what I prayed. But surely this little prayer has been abundantly answered. In my service for Him I discovered year after year that to glorify Christ is the only true ministry of the Spirit of God. The passion of the new life is the passion which filled the great Apostle's soul—"Not I, but Christ." With me it has been a steady, growing passion, and more and more, I have learned the meaning of Peter's beautiful words: "Whom having not seen, ye love, in whom, though now ye see Him not, yet believing, ye rejoice with joy unspeakable and full of glory." (I Pet. 1:8.) To exalt the Lord Jesus Christ, to glorify His Name, to worship and adore Him, has become the passion of my life.

I do not remember a Bible Conference, or a visit just for a day to a new place, when I did not select for the first sermon something relating to Himself. Once, leaving a Sunday morning service, following the people, I overheard one person saying, "That certainly was disappointing; I thought this preacher coming from New York would tell us something about what is going on there, and all he preached was about Jesus." This person revealed the spiritual leanness, if not death, of his soul.

J. H. Sammis, the author of "Trust and Obey," came to me one Sunday morning in the "Church of the Open Door" in Los Angeles, and said after my sermon, "I love to hear you preach, for you exalt my Lord. This morning your message has given me a new and greater glimpse of Himself.

Thank you!" Christ ministered to Christians supplies the need all believers have. Such ministry brings peace and joy, comfort and strength, power and blessing, to the souls of men. The most oratorical flight of a modernist leaves the hearts dead and empty; and so does the preaching which does not give to the Lord Jesus Christ the place of preeminence.

To exalt our Lord and delight ourselves in Him constitutes our fellowship with the Father. It secures the presence and the power of the Holy Spirit. According to the words of our Lord the Holy Spirit in His coming "shall not speak of Himself. . . . He shall glorify Me, for He shall receive of Mine, and shall show it unto you" (John xvi:13, 14). Sects and cults which speak constantly of the Spirit and His inward operations, and put the Lord Jesus Christ and His work into the background, are not governed by the Holy Spirit. Another significant fact is that these extravagant movements, calling themselves "Apostolic" or "Pentecostal" with counterfeit gifts, always speak of our Lord as "Jesus." The full title which belongs to Him, "the Lord Jesus Christ," is not used by them. In the light of 1 Corinthians xii:3 this is significant indeed; no man can say that Jesus is Lord, but by the Holy Spirit. And hence, where the Lordship of Christ is not emphasized, the Holy Spirit's presence may be questioned.

On the cover of *Our Hope* is printed 1 Timothy i:1, "The Lord Jesus Christ, who is our Hope." I am convinced that this monthly testimony has been sustained for almost forty years, because it aims at the glory of our blessed Lord. How often it has come to my heart that this exaltation of the Lord is the highest and best I could do.

And how manifold and inexhaustible is this theme! No tongue nor pen can describe the glory of Him, "whose goings forth have been from of old, from everlasting." While my messages covered all phases of His glory and all phases of His precious work, I have been led to stress His future glory, which will be His in the day of His personal and visible return. As the reader has learned, the truth of the Lord's Coming came to me when I began the work among the Jews. Prophetic truths came to me gradually. I learned from Scripture that there is a hope for Israel. The restoration promises given by the various prophets of the Lord are still awaiting a future fulfilment. Besides a national restoration to their God-given land, the promises of God announce a future regeneration, when the remnant of the nation will have a rebirth, when the heart of stone will be taken away, and they will be circumcised in heart. The laws of a logical and sound exegesis demand a literal fulfilment of all these promises.

Then I discovered next, that this regeneration

and restoration cannot be accomplished apart
from the Second Advent of our Lord. The unfulfilled promises of Israel await His visible and
glorious return. Furthermore, I found in Scripture
that His return will be preceded by the time of
Jacob's trouble, called in Daniel's prophecy "a
time of trouble, such as never was since there was
a nation even to that same time" (Dan. xii:1).
And our Lord speaks of it likewise in the still unful-
fulfilled Olivet discourse (Matt. xxiv) and calls it
"the great tribulation." The next truth, which
was given to me through the study of His Word,
was the truth concerning the Church, the Body
and the Bride of Christ, and that blessed Hope,
which is only revealed in the New Testament
(1 Thess. iv:16-18). I learned to distinguish
between the Coming of the Lord *for* His Saints,
and His Coming *with* His Saints. The prophetic
portions of God's Holy Word became then my
specialty. Many Christians seem to believe that
the Lord has bestowed upon me a special gift in
unfolding these truths to the people of God.

It is certainly a much needed message, and meat
in due season for the household of faith. The Lord
has used me with hundreds of Christians through
my spoken messages, and much more through my
books, in opening up to their hearts this neglected
portion of the Bible. As it is known, Satan has
done his best to link some of the most soul-destroy-
ing errors with the teaching of prophecy. Such

vicious systems as Mormonism, Spiritism, Russellism (International Bible Student's Association) and others, all speak of the second Coming of Christ. On the other hand, the professing Church has ignored, and almost totally neglected, the study of unfulfilled prophecy. Teaching prophecy, as I have done all these years, has often brought me ridicule. And frequently certain ignorant people scattered the report that I am a Seventh Day Adventist, a Millerite, or a Russellite. The teachers or the institutions who seek popularity and support from the religious world, should avoid teaching the premillennial eschatology. Some, I am sorry to say, who used to teach these dispensational truths, are giving them up, and some are even antagonistic. Such a course is dishonoring to the Lord and to His Word. It will not result in blessing. So long as He permits me to serve, I shall continue to preach the full Gospel. The preaching which leaves out "that blessed Hope," which neglects the preaching of the glory which awaits sinners saved by grace in the day of His manifestation, is only a half Gospel.

Once more in this closing chapter of a servant's autobiography, I wish to mention prayer. It is more important than preaching and teaching. The Spirit-filled Apostles spoke rightly when they said: "But we will give ourselves continually to prayer, and to the ministery of the Word" (Acts vi:4). They put prayer first. True ministry must be born in prayer and communion with the Lord. A ministry without prayer is barren. Nor is it the duty of the servant only to pray much, to pray continually, but all the children of God must pray for the ministry. Often I have felt the difference in holding my meetings. In one place it seemed so hard to speak the Word; it seemed almost as if I were up against a solid, stone wall. Then I came to another town, and as soon as I began, I had great liberty and great blessing. The one place was prayerless; in the other the people had prayed for weeks for a blessing, and the expected blessing came with the first service held.

It must be the servant's constant prayer to be guided in His service, not only as to the places to be visited, but also as to the messages. Many times I have sat in a pulpit with my Bible in hand, having my fingers in two or three places, undecided what text to take and praying that I might select the right message for waiting hearts. The Lord is the Head of the Body; the servants of Christ are members of the Body, each is put in a special place, with a special gift and service. As the head of the physical body directs every member of the body, so the Lord Jesus directs the members of His Body. "Lord, what wilt Thou have me to do?" is the true servant's prayer. All this is the expression of the servant's utter dependence on His Lord. How I have enjoyed, and how I am enjoying, this blessed dependence on Him, the Lord of all!

A brief word about the support of the servant. One who is really called of the Lord and goes forth in His Name, does not need to worry about his support. The Lord whom he serves will be mindful of him, and supply his need. The Lord Himself has ordained "that they which preach the Gospel, should live of the Gospel" (1 Corinthians ix:14). The definite command is given, "Let him that is taught in the Word communicate unto him that teacheth in all good things" (Gal. vi:6). But if the servant looks to man, or uses certain methods, or schemes, to secure funds, he will be disappointed. Man always disappoints; the Lord never.

Many letters have reached me in my ministry asking for terms. "What are your terms? How much do you charge?" I have no terms and make no definite charges. On different occasions during different years, when people wrote that they might furnish entertainment and part of the traveling expenses, covered by free-will offerings, and nothing more, I gladly went to minister the Gospel. Then on my return home letters came from some of His stewards inclosing personal fellowship to encourage me in my ministry. And these brethren did not know the circumstances. Such experiences make the Lord very real. But the servant of Christ is not exempt from obeying the exhortation, "But to do good and to communicate forget not; for with such sacrifices God is well pleased"

(Heb. xiii:16). For over twenty years it has been my happy privilege to set aside from my ministry, personal fellowships and other incomes, certain sums, to which gifts of others were added, in a special donation account. Many thousands of dollars have been devoted in this way to missionary purposes, the free circulation of literature in different languages, the support of individuals, and of late the Stony Brook School. In this good work I continue, tasting a little of the sweetness of His saying, "It is more blessed to give than to receive" (Acts xx:35).

A half of a century's ministry is a long time. The question naturally arises, "How much longer?" The last chapter in the Gospel of John gives the answer. Here the Lordship of the Lord Jesus Christ is seen in directing the service of His servants; in supplying their physical need; in restoring the servant who had failed and denied Him, and finally in ordering the arranging of their departure out of this life. To Peter the Lord revealed that it was His will that he should grow old, and then the manner of his death would be crucifixion. Concerning John the Lord said in rebuking Peter's inquisitiveness, "If I will that he tarry till I come, what is that to thee?"

The Lord who calls His servants, who guides them, sustains and keeps them, also knows when and how to terminate their service. John Wesley spoke truly, when he said as to a servant of Christ,

"We are immortal as long as our work is not done." And so I often say, "I go on serving, ready to go wherever He leads, as long as it pleases Him."

And as one gets older and older in this service, there is no need to speak, as is so often done, of declining years. True faith knows no declining years. The years of old age are for faith, ascending years. The promises of God are not limited to certain years of human existence. I intend to continue to claim Isaiah xl:31, "They that wait upon the Lord shall renew their strength; they shall mount up with wings as eagles; they shall run and not be weary; they shall walk and not faint." The verse of my life, "Call upon me in the day of trouble: I will deliver thee and thou shalt glorify Me," will still be used, though years come and go. Of course, it is true that the outward man, as age comes on, declines. But it is also written, "But though our outward man perish, yet the inward man is renewed day by day."

The forward look of the servant of Christ is most glorious. The Bible, especially the New Testament, does not authorize us to say that death, and with death the promised reward crowns, is the goal of the servant. Of late a certain company developing a new cemetery has repeatedly urged me to invest in a good-sized lot. I felt like writing them that I have no money to invest in a cemetery lot. I believe in 1 Corinthians xv:51 and 52, "Behold I show you a mystery: we shall not all sleep, but we shall be changed, in a moment, in the twinkling of an eye, at the last trump; for the trumpet shall sound, and the dead shall be raised incorruptible, and we shall be changed." And this may be the happy lot of every living believer. Who knows how soon this promise may pass into history? Certainly the signs of the times are most significant, indicating as never before the near-ending of our age. And with this thought I occupy till He comes; I toil on till Lord and servant meet face to face.

A certain liberalist, having written his autobiography, ended by speaking of the great adventure, death, which he felt would soon come to him. And then he expressed doubt as to where he was going, and where the adventure would lead him. That is how some modernists pass on, unless they lay hold, before the silver cord breaks, on the Cross and find there the assurance and the hope which the soul needs.

My hope is sure, and there is no uncertainty as to my destiny. I know I shall meet the Lord, who guided me as a boy, who kept me as a youth, who called me to service, who sustained and upheld me throughout these years. It thrills my whole being when I think of the verse, "I shall see Him as He is." I shall meet Him in the Father's house; I shall be like Him; I shall share His glory, and I shall be forever with the Lord.

Many times I have read His words and pon-

241

dered over their meaning, "If any man serve Me, let him follow Me; and where I am, there also my servant shall be; if any man serve Me, him my Father will honor" (John xii:26). What honor, then, awaits the servant of Christ?

Will my service end when He comes, or will there be some higher service? It is a blessed mystery. Yet I read of the New Jerusalem, where His servants will be gathered, "His servants shall serve Him" (Rev. xxii:3). What service will it be?

Are there other worlds to be visited? Worlds, where sin too has wrought its awful havoc? Is service needed there? Who knows? It is a mystery. We see but into a glass darkly. We must wait until the day comes when we shall know as we are known.

Thousands have heard from my lips of clay about that coming day. It has become for me year after year a greater reality, and now often homesickness for that day, which will bring us all home, comes into my heart.

And what a day it will be, when we shall see Him! What a day it will be when in His own presence we shall receive the promised rewards! What a day when we can worship Him by casting our crowns at His feet! What a day of praise and glory! What a day when the flock of God is gathered home to be forever with the great Shepherd of the sheep!

What a meeting it will be ! All the saints will be there. They will all be one. Not one will claim a denominational name, or boast in a Cephas, a Paul, an Apollos, a Luther, or in the four Johns: John Calvin, John Knox, John Wesley, or John Darby. Christ will be all and in all. And if this is the happy goal, why not have this happiness here?

And so I serve still, as it pleases Him. And so I wait, while I serve, for the glorious day of His appearing.

INDEX

245

INDEX

INDEX

Galveston, Texas, 185 ff.
Gates, Mrs. Gertrude Lewis, 200
Genesis, 92, 176, 196, 230
Georgia, 136
German, 29, 54, 90, 96, 106, 126, 130, 131, 168, 194, 199, 209
Germantown, Pa., 128
Germany, 1, 2, 126, 217
Ghetto, (N. Y.), 33, 67, 82
Gift of Tongues, 160, 177
Gloversville, N. Y., 121
Goldstein, Samuel, 18, 19, 20
Gonzales, Texas, 194
Goodman, Mr. and Mrs. H. B., 188
Gordon, Dr. A. J., 39, 45, 104, 153
Gordon, Mr. and Mrs. Amos K., 122, 123, 139
Gordon, Dr. Charles W. (Ralph Connor), 179
Gorham, N. H., 105
Gospel, 1, 2, 3, 9, 10, 17, 19, 20, 40, 41, 47, 50, 63, 70, 96, 101, 102, 108, 119, 126, 130, 131, 137, 146, 151, 153, 159, 179, 186, 189, 192, 202, 208, 218, 224, 227, 229, 236, 238
Govan, Saskatchewan, 181
Grace Reformed Episcopal Church, Scranton, 48
Grand Canyon, 201
Grand Forks, N. D., 167
Grand Rapids, Mich., 150
Grandview, Iowa, 157, 158
Granite City, Ill., 153
Grant, F. W., 85
Gray, Dr. James M., 70, 71, 92, 105, 110, 114, 151, 180
Great Britain, 217
Great Northern Railroad, 174, 175
Greek Orthodox Church, 59
Green Street Presbyterian Church, Baltimore, 133

Greenwich, Conn., 106
Gregory, Dr. G. H., 37
Gremmels, Charles E., 114
Griepenberg, Count of, 59
Grimm, Rev. C. F., 14
Grimm, Emma F. (Mrs. A. C. Gaebelein), 14, 15, 18, 25, 41, 123, 142, 143
Grosvenor, Jonothan Prescott, 106
Grosvenor, Pauline, 106
Grove City, Pa., 128
Groveland, Ill., 153
Gzowski, C., 143, 144
Guers, Pastor, 5
Guille, Dr. George, 180
Guiness, Dr. Grattan, 164
Gull Lake, Mich., 151

Hall, William Philips, 115
Hallock, Minn., 167
Ham, Rev. Mordecai F., 186, 194
Hamilton, Ontario, 145, 146
Hamilton Square Baptist Church, San Francisco, 211
Hamilton, Rev. William, 25
Harbison, Mr. and Mrs. S. P., 45
Harcus, Sinclair, 150
Harlan, Iowa, 157
Harlem Methodist Church, New York City, 13 ff.
Harmony of the Prophetic Word, The, 88, 204
Harris, Dr. Elmore, 71, 145, 154
Harrisburg, Pa., 47, 127
Harrower, C. S., 37
Hartford Ave. M. E. Church, Baltimore, 9, 10
Hartford, Conn., 106
Harvard University, 118
Haslup, Leroy, 130
Haupt, Professor Paul, 11

251

INDEX

INDEX

INDEX

TITLES IN THIS SERIES

The Evangelical Matrix
1875-1900

■ 10. Arthur T. Pierson, ed.
The Inspired Word: A Series of Papers and
Addresses Delivered at the Bible Inspiration Conference,
Philadelphia, 1887
London, 1888

■ 11. Moody Bible Institute Correspondence
Dept. *First Course — Bible Doctrines, Instructor—*
R. A. Torrey; Eight Sections with Questions,
Chicago, 1901

The Formation of
A Fundamentalist Agenda
1900-1920

■ 12. Amzi C. Dixon,
Evangelism Old and New,
New York, 1905

■ 13. William Bell Riley
The Finality of the Higher Criticism;
or, The Theory of Evolution and False Theology
Minneapolis, 1909

■ 14.-17 George M. Marsden, ed.
The Fundamentals: A Testimony to the Truth
New York, 1988

Fundamentalism Versus Modernism
1920-1935

■ 24. Joel A. Carpentar, ed.
Modernism and Foreign Missions:
Two Fundamentalist Protests
New York, 1988

■ 25. John Horsch
Modern Religious Liberalism: The Destructiveness
and Irrationality of Modernist Theology
Scottsdale, Pa., 1921

■ 26. Joel A. Carpenter,ed.
Fundamentalist vesus Modernist
The Debates Between
John Roach Stratton and Charles Francis Potter
New York, 1988

■ 27. Joel A. Carpenter, ed.
William Jennings Bryan on
Orthodoxy, Modernism, and Evolution
New York, 1988

■ 28. Edwin H. Rian
The Presbyterian Conflict
Grand Rapids, 1940

Sectarian Fundamentalism
1930-1950

■ 29. Arno C. Gaebelein
Half a Century: The Autobiography of a Servant
New York, 1930

■ 30. Charles G. Trumball
Prophecy's Light on Today
New York, 1937

■ 31. Joel A. Carpenter, ed.
Biblical Prophecy in an Apocalyptic Age:
Selected Writings of Louis S. Bauman
New York, 1988

■ 32. Joel A. Carpenter, ed.
Fighting Fundamentalism:
Polemical Thrusts of the 1930s and 1940s
New York, 1988

■ 33. *Inside History of First Baptist Church, Fort*
Worth, and Temple Baptist Church, Detroit:
Life Story of Dr. J. Frank Norris
Fort Worth, 1938

■ 34. John R. Rice
The Home — Courtship, Marriage, and Children: A
Biblical Manual of Twenty -Two Chapters
on the Christian Home.

Wheaton, 1945

■ 35. Joel A. Carpenter, ed.
Good Books and the Good Book: Reading Lists by
Wilbur M. Smith, Fundamentalist Bibliophile
New York, 1988

■ 36. H. A. Ironside
Random Reminiscences from Fifty Years of Ministry
New York, 1939

■ 37 Joel A. Carpenter,ed.
*Sacrificial Lives: Young Martyrs
and Fundamentalist Idealism*
New York, 1988.

Rebuilding, Regrouping, & Revival
1930-1950

■ 38. J. Elwin Wright
*The Old Fashioned Revival Hour
and the Broadcasters*
Boston, 1940

■ 39. Joel A. Carpenter, ed.
*Enterprising Fundamentalism:
Two Second-Generation Leaders*
New York, 1988

■ 40. Joel A. Carpenter, ed.
Missionary Innovation and Expansion
New York, 1988

■ 41. Joel A. Carpenter, ed.
*A New Evangelical Coalition: Early Documents
of the National Association of Evangelicals*
New York, 1988

■ 42. Carl McIntire
Twentieth Century Reformation
Collingswood, N. J., 1944